MODERN BRIDE
Guide to Your Wedding and Marriage

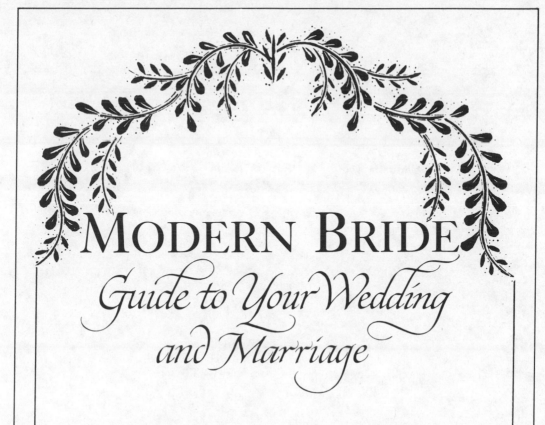

MODERN BRIDE
Guide to Your Wedding and Marriage

The Editors of *Modern Bride*
with
Stephanie H. Dahl

Foreword by Cele Goldsmith Lalli
Illustrations by JoAnn Wanamaker

Ballantine Books · New York

Library of Congress Catalog Card Number: 84-90818
ISBN 0-345-31508-1
Cover photograph by Tito Barberis
Book Design by Amy Lamb
Charts designed by Anita Karl and James Kemp

Manufactured in the United States of America

First Edition: November 1984

10 9 8 7 6 5 4 3

Acknowledgments

We wish to thank the following individuals for so graciously sharing their time and experience: Laura Behn; Judy Crane; Clifford and Aaron Dahl; Michael and Diane DiNapoli; Jules, Harriet, and Elizabeth Erwin; Bobby and Ginger Glander; Jospehine Hargrett; Rosa Lee Harker; Patricia Helstern; Michael, Francesca, and Erica Lalli; Michael Martin; Charles and Diana Measter; Joseph and Malinda Mylek; Georgana Repal; Stephen and Shirley Ritchie; Robert Sappio; and Eleanor Schoepflin.

We also gratefully acknowledge the following for their professional expertise: Janet Brown/Egan, Janet Brown/Egan Consultant to the Bride; Eleanor Brzozka, The Inverness Country Club; Ida Davidoff, Ed.D., Albert Einstein College of Medicine; David Goldfarb, SNAG, Design Studios; Rabbi Mark S. Golub, Executive Director of Jewish Education in Media, Inc.; Roy F. Guste, Jr., Antoine's Restaurant; David Holtz, Eastman-Kodak Company; Kermit Kasse, Antoine's Restaurant; Frank Labbancz, Saint Leo's Roman Catholic Church; Rabbi Aaron Landes, Beth Sholom Congregation; Reverend Constantine Mathews, Annunciation Greek Orthodox Church; Franklin Melzer, J.D.; George E. Morrissey, Publisher, *Modern Bride* Magazine; Stella Mostel, M.S., Stamford Center for Human Sexuality; Lorenzo Pizzia, The Mark Hopkins Hotel; Nannette Poillon, Connecticut Connection Realty, Inc.; Ilene S. Rogers, J.D.; Pearl Smith, Art Wedding Service, Inc.; Chaplain, Captain Mark J. Spence, U.S.A.F.; Anne Tobin-Ashe, Ed.D., Georgetown University; Reverend Robert E. Weiss, Saint Leo's Roman Catholic Church; and Sandy Zweben, The Shadowbrook.

Also the following groups and organizations: American Bar Association, Chicago, Illinois; Buddhist Vidhartha Society, Washington, D.C.; Hindu Vidanta Society, New York, New York; Interstate Commerce Commission, Washington, D.C.; National Association of Realtors, Washington, D.C.; and National Association of Home Builders, Washington, D.C.

Finally, our gratitude to *Modern Bride* staff members Carolyn Bartel, Sandra K. Boles, Jacqueline Bondy, Guillaume Bruneau, Mary Ann Cavlin, Susan H. Freiman, Bruce Klein, Jacqueline McCord Leo, and Melanie Kubat Rush.

Contents

PART TWO: YOUR WEDDING

PART THREE: YOUR MARRIAGE

Foreword

As a young woman making plans to be married, you're probably most excited about creating the wedding of your dreams. You'll rush out to buy *Modern Bride* primarily to see the newest designs in wedding attire and you won't be disappointed—the latest fashions for brides, maids, men, and moms will be there in abundance. Romantic honeymoon destinations will beckon, and much of what you need for you first home will be beautifully displayed. You'll curl up with your fiancé for hours of pleasant planning, and the magazine will be your personal pictorial guide for the biggest and best buying spree of your lives.

This is important and certainly thrilling, but it should not take priority over the most essential consideration: your relationship with each other. Is it solid enough to weather the challenge of life together? Marriage requires emotional maturity. You need to feel secure about your own identity and comfortable with yourself before you can share a lifetime with another human being. The same is true for your fiancé. With thorough self-knowledge you can begin to explore together the many questions that have to be answered about your expectations as individuals and as a couple. For example: how will you manage your home, two careers, financial matters, in-laws? Do you want children? Does he? Can you both handle that responsibility? And much, much more.

We cannot emphasize strongly enough the necessity for thoroughly exploring your backgrounds, familial and cultural attitudes, and all other areas affecting interpersonal behavior. There is no better time to do this than during your engagement. While you are planning the perfect wedding, do spend at least as much time and energy working on a firm intellectual and emotional foundation for your marriage.

A large part of this book is devoted to helping you do this. Through features adapted from *Modern Bride*, new research, interviews with clergy, professional marriage counselors, and couples, it brings you a compendium of experience and information never before available in one volume. Along with complete advice on every aspect of traditional and contemporary wedding planning, you will find the guidance and resources necessary to evaluate your readiness for marriage knowledgeably and honestly.

It is our sincere hope that your wedding day will be the beautiful beginning of a loving, mutually fulfilling lifetime partnership.

Cele Goldsmith Lalli
Editor in Chief
Modern Bride Magazine

Introduction
What Is A Wedding?

A wedding is a study in contrasts. It is a public profession of intensely private feelings, an outward symbol of an inner commitment. It is a ritual at once emotional, theatrical, sentimental, spiritual, and legal. It indulges our wildest fantasies of the perfect wedding, yet it demands great judgment in coping with less than perfect reality. Perhaps no other occasion requires more sensitivity in balancing the ideal and the real, the surface and the substance, than our own wedding.

Moreover, a wedding is not something in and of itself, but merely a prelude to a much greater reality: the ongoing state of married life. What is it we cherish about the celebration of a twenty-fifth or fiftieth wedding anniversary? Certainly not the anniversary party itself. Rather it is our recognition of the commitment, the sharing, the compromise, and the strength of two people who have worked at their lives together that gives us joy.

We all know what a task it is to achieve day-to-day harmony with our co-workers, our neighbors, and our families. Yet amazingly, in a world fraught with suspicion and discord, we continue to seek personal partnerships and alliances, to "take a chance on love." Perhaps that is the greatest testament to the beauty and spirit of humankind. A wedding celebrates this willingness to risk hurt and disappointment in pursuit of the deep fulfillment of conjugal love.

Time was when the ideal of love and the reality of love were much more in accord. When a couple fell in love, they got married. Every bride was young, naive, and virginal; every groom was eager, responsible, and assured; every family was protective, concerned, and supportive. They all hailed from the same background and believed in the same God. The march down the aisle was the ritualistic beginning of a predictable life together. Because the cast of characters was fairly stereotyped, at least in theory, the rules of the nuptial ceremony and the expectations of married life were hardly ever questioned.

But along came America, the blending of diverse cultures and the evolution of a new society. Our strong individualism and our common-sense adaptability challenged Old World social customs with new needs. Americans continue to seek the best of both worlds, the old and the new, with characteristic ingenuity. The result is a unique culture of our own, indebted as it may be to those of our forefathers, and we will no longer accept institutions and mores that restrict, rather than reflect, our national character.

Consider first the changing profile of our cast of characters. A recent study of Newlywed Reader Service inquirers to *Modern Bride* reveals that the average bride and groom are older: twenty-four and twenty-six respectively; better educated: 80 percent of all brides and 76 percent of all grooms have attended college; and generally more sophisticated: almost half of all brides and grooms hold professional positions and 39 percent own residences. The 1980 Census confirms that 30 percent of the 25 million marriages taking place in the eighties are not first marriages, and that nearly 2 million American couples are cohabiting outside of wedlock.

To a more mature cast, add the following social variables: Many brides and grooms are the children of divorced parents, extended family situations, or multinational backgrounds. Economic conditions may necessitate the bride and groom assuming some of the wedding expenses, and both contributing to the lifestyle they hope to establish. Families and friends are often as involved in their own lives and careers as the bride and groom are, and have little time to help plan weddings or offer advice. In our highly mobile society, parents, relatives, friends, and even prospective spouses may be scattered all over the globe, and plans must often be made via long distance.

In short, the whole connotation of a wedding has changed. Whereas the ceremonies once reflected the culture and affluence of the families involved, they now tend to reflect the lifestyle of the couple. Having once served as the official beginning of a marital relationship, weddings now often acknowledge a lifetime commitment that has already been made, never mind consummated. Our busy society's preference for at-home entertaining and for economy of time and money has prevailed in new attitudes of social acceptability. And while there is still, to be sure, a correct way to do things, the range of rightness has broadened considerably to accommodate a myriad of circumstances.

It is important to remember, too, that with today's lifestyle options, people no longer *have* to get married; they *choose* to get married. And, interestingly enough, more people are choosing marriage every year. There is in all of us a need to belong, to feel secure, to create a family. The fact that marriage is in style again reflects the renewed realization of those needs. For more mature brides and grooms who have become disenchanted with the single life or disillusioned by unfulfilling relationships, there is a need for the wedding to recapture some of its traditional significance, to represent their faith in the endurance of the married state.

The basic premise of this book is that American society *has* changed. To refuse to address certain irregular situations or to face some unexpected difficulties is to be totally unrealistic in our expectations of both the wedding ceremony and the marriage. Words like *etiquette, commitment, responsibility,* even *love,* may be rather old-fashioned, but they do not have to be irrelevant to contemporary American life.

For all their disparities in age, location, finances, and personal situations, modern couples still have one thing in common: each wants their marriage to be successful and their wedding day to be as lovely and as memorable as they can make it. Even in a changing society, these goals can be accomplished.

MODERN BRIDE
Guide to Your Wedding and Marriage

*Part One
Your Engagement*

Making the Decision

*M*arriage. Everybody has an opinion on it and some advice to offer those about to enter into it. But with it all, one is ultimately left alone with the decision.

Why do people marry? Recent nationwide surveys show that "love" remains the most common response given to that question. But what is love? Are there not as many definitions of love as there are people? What is the special kind of love that makes people want to marry, rather than merely be friends or lovers?

Modern psychology and sociology have contributed greatly to a better understanding of the real meaning of love. Gone are the fairy-tale dreams of a frail princess being whisked away by a knight in shining armor. Gone, too, are the notions of obedience, submission, and happily ever after. Only the most devout romanticist would proclaim to love at first sight; how can one profess to love what one does not know?

Most of us, through simple trial and error, have discovered the difference between the initial experience of falling or being in love and the more permanent state of loving. Yet we still overlook the conscious act of will involved in the loving process. In his landmark book *The Art of Loving*, Eric Fromm explains the distinction this way:

> To love somebody is not just a strong feeling—it is a decision, it is a judgment, it is a promise. If love were only a feeling, there would be no basis for the promise to love each other forever. A feeling

comes and it may go. How can I judge that it will stay forever, when
my act does not involve judgment and decision?[1]

To decide to marry is to decide to love: to decide that you can and will cherish
this person for the rest of your life.

All this is not to say that the romance has gone out of love. Certainly, modern
lovers still write poetry, send flowers, and dine by candlelight, but the emotion
from which these impulses spring is more reasoned, more realistic. Rather than
making us helpless victims, we expect love to liberate us from our endless search
for security and companionship. Our idea of married love includes friendship,
freedom, compatibility, communication, sharing, and stability. Ironically, the
broader interpretations of love and the greater expectations of the love relationship
have probably contributed to today's higher divorce rate. People will simply no
longer accept what they can change—not for love or money!

In spite of the proliferation of divorce in our society, individual acceptance of
it falls far short of the practice. The stigma of failure remains, and no reasonable
person would ever enter into a marriage expecting that marriage to end in the
courts. Precisely this attitude inhibits the widespread use of marital contracts and
prenuptial agreements. We believe that marriage should be more than a property
settlement, and that "what God has joined together, let no man put asunder."

Now that you have made the decision to marry, you are probably determined
as never before not to become another divorce statistic. I know I love him, you
may say to yourself, but am I doing the right thing? Am I marrying for the right
reasons? What can I do now, during the engagement, to ensure that my marriage
will get off to a good start?

There's actually a lot you can do now—mainly by sorting through your own
thoughts about marriage and discussing them with your fiancé. It's important to
understand each other's basic notions about what marriage is in order to work
toward common goals and to create a relationship that satisfies both of you. If
there are going to be areas of disagreement, it is best to know about them now to
avoid misunderstanding and disillusionment later on. Together you can strive to
resolve any difficulties from the very beginning.

Much of this first section is designed to help you start thinking about these basic
issues. Even if your fiancé has no interest in the other aspects of wedding preparation, we urge you to share this part of the book with him and to talk about it
together. The more you know about each other before the wedding, the smoother
your early months and years together will be.

Family Background and Expectations of Marriage

The home from which you come is the foundation of your values, your lifestyle,
and your expectations. It is the first source of self-knowledge and often the only

source of family preparation and training. If your home life was happy due to a solid relationship between your parents, you are likely to desire a similar relationship for yourself. If your home was troubled by arguments or separation, you may be wary, but you may also resolve to do things differently and more successfully. Regardless of the quality of past experiences, fully 90 percent of the population will marry at some point in life, and the majority of those who marry will have children.[2]

A study by the Institute of Social Research at the University of Michigan found that 97 percent of eighteen-year-olds questioned in 1980 expected to marry.[3] A more recent survey by *Seventeen* magazine indicates that 93 percent of their female teenage respondents expect to marry someday. Eight out of ten plan to take their husband's last name, 73 percent want a large, religious wedding, and all plan to continue a career after marriage.[4] Evidently these young women have been thinking about their eventual marriages for quite some time.

As a matter of fact, most young women do. Adolescent girls fantasize about the romance of falling in love and the splendor of their weddings. They play silly games designed to reveal the future, and worry about whether Mr. Right will ever come along. But as they near adulthood, such childish fantasies are replaced by a new awareness of what makes marriage work. Expectations regarding the type of relationship and the quality of family life become much more specific, even though a prospective spouse is not on the scene.

Liz, a thoughtful college senior, provides an example: "I may not choose the exact lifestyle my parents have chosen over the years, but I do want the same kind of relationship they have. I admire their loyalty, their laughter, their individual strengths. When I think about a husband of my own, I don't picture him in a physical sense, although I assume I will find him attractive, but I picture him more as a type—a family man, an honest, affectionate person whom I can respect and who will respect me. I don't anticipate a problem-free life, but I do expect that we will be able to confront our problems and to adapt to whatever comes our way."

From Liz's comments, we sense that hers is a close-knit, affectionate family. It may not always be without conflicts, but it is one in which openness, respect, and humor prevail. In expecting to re-create the same atmosphere in her own home one day, Liz has already identified certain character traits in a mate which she considers intrinsic to a solid marriage and a happy family. Such traits carry an implied assumption of shared values and mutual goals within an overall willingness to adapt and compromise.

The importance of family background as a determining force in our own values, expectations, and lifestyles cannot be underestimated. Indeed, the entire concept of family therapy is based on the continuation of family patterns and systems from one generation to the next. Marriage blends not only two personalities but two families. And the reality, though young lovers may not want to hear it, is that we marry not only a spouse but also the parents and the whole family tree!

Understanding family systems and genealogies helps us understand ourselves and others. The whole family, taken as a unit with aunts, uncles, cousins, grandparents, and everyone else, projects a singular approach to certain life issues. Why does your family celebrate weddings or funerals in a specific way? How does it handle monetary or household responsibilities? What are the feelings toward sex, religion, politics? What are the relationships between you and your parents, between your brothers and sisters? Most importantly, whether the family is your own or your fiancé's, how do you accept or reject these attitudes?

All of this is a great deal more than simply a question of ethnic origin, religion, or income. Even in families that may seem similar on the surface, fundamental attitudes about family life can be very different. Ask yourself questions such as the following about your own family, and ask your fiancé to do the same about his; then compare notes. Once you start thinking along these lines, many other questions about your respective families will come to mind, questions worthy of discussion.

- How do your parents treat their parents? Is there a respect for cultural and/or religious traditions? Are older relatives valued and generational ties viewed with pride?
- What is the atmosphere of your home? Are family members open and demonstrative or private and reticent? How interdependent are they?
- How are day-to-day decisions made? Who makes important long-term decisions? What roles did children have in family decision making?
- Were you raised permissively or strictly? What responsibilities did you have in the home? What areas of your performance were considered most important: schoolwork? sports? employment? behavior? social life? appearance?
- How are rights and responsibilities divided? Did your mother work outside the home? Did your father share household chores and child care? Were there rigid sex-role stereotypes?
- Are there frequent arguments at home? If so, what about? How do family members show anger, disappointment, or hurt?
- Does your family spend leisure time together? Are friends valued as an important part of family life? Do your parents socialize predominantly as a couple? Did you go with them on vacations as a child?
- Are there any taboos in your household? Any prejudices? Are you ashamed of any family member?

The analysis of family background, if done honestly, can provide a valuable source of self-knowledge and a reasonable gauge of behavior in other situations. An understanding of your family's strengths will prepare you to cultivate them in your own marriage; an understanding of its weaknesses will equip you to guard against those problems. And by comparing your analysis with your fiancé's, you can anticipate some of the adjustments you will both have to make as you create your own family.

"Getting to Know You": The Function of the Engagement

Taking a critical look at your family can help you define what you want from marriage. But to determine if *this* marriage has a chance to satisfy those needs, you have to take a critical look at your fiancé—and at your relationship with him.

Unfortunately, this is difficult to do when you've been bitten by the love bug. Right now your fiancé probably seems pretty close to perfect. Sad to say, he isn't— he's just an ordinary human being, albeit a wonderful one. At the point when things are serious, during the period of pre-engagement or early engagement, some good sense must temper faith and love, and the feasibility of a lifetime commitment to this special person must be ascertained.

"Mike is the one," says Tricia, twenty, of her fiancé. "I guess I knew it three or four months after we started going out. We like the same things, we come from similar families, we have the same religion. It scared me because I really wasn't looking for anything serious in my life. Then I found myself hoping he would propose, then petrified that he would propose, then wondering what we'd do if he did. He's twenty-six, out of college, and ready to settle down. I have school to finish and would like to exert a little independence first, but how long can I expect him to wait?"

Mike is not only a good bit older than Tricia, but he is also, as it turns out, old enough to know what he wants and to be willing to wait for it. "An education was important to me," says Mike, "and I feel it's important for Tricia. Two years is not a very long time to wait for what's right. Besides, we are still together. We can use the time to get to know each other better and to plan our lives."

Actually, two years is proving to be just barely enough engagement time for Tricia and Mike. Because they live in the heavily populated Northeast, they have found preferred reception sites for a December wedding booked a year and a half to two years in advance. And, both being Roman Catholic, they have found that their diocese requires a year's notification in order to be able to complete mandatory prenuptial programs. What with working and parties and shopping and school and general wedding planning, Mike and Tricia already find themselves scheduling weeks and months in advance to attend to the necessities of arranging their lives together.

On top of that, Tricia still needs some time to deal with the whole situation, to get used to the idea of "moving out of my father's house into my husband's." While she comes from a traditional family with traditional values, Tricia is also a very modern young woman intent on preserving her personhood and individuality. A long engagement affords her the time to adjust emotionally and psychologically to marrying sooner than she had expected.

It is to Mike's credit that he is able to recognize their differences in readiness as well as in age, and to balance his love with patience and understanding. As a couple, Tricia and Mike seem to have an exceptionally clear perception of the magnitude of their commitment to each other, and the maturity to utilize their engagement period to strengthen that commitment into a firm basis for marriage.

"Aha," you say, "this is a pitch for long engagements!" Not necessarily. But it *is* a pitch for long marriages. And the way to achieve a long marriage is by allowing yourself enough time to know what you are getting into *before* you have gotten into it.

Granted, a considerable commitment has already been made at the time the engagement is formalized. The very act of betrothal is in itself a pledge or a promise to deliver one's work, one's loyalty, one's self. But the word *engage* is also used to mean encounter, as to engage in conversation—or in battle. Interestingly enough, the second usage may offer the best insight into what a formal period of engagement is really all about.

The document signed in a solemnized engagement ceremony states that the couple is "to prepare in faith and love" to enter into the state of matrimony.[5] Inherent in this statement is the responsibility to learn more about each other, to attempt to resolve any areas of discord, and to abandon the commitment to marry only for the most serious reasons and irreconcilable doubts. Such goals would seem valid for all reasonable couples, whether betrothed in a ceremony or not, as they rightly delineate the preparation for marriage as the single most important task to be undertaken during the engagement period.

To engage each other in honest conversation, to encounter likeness and dissimilarity, to conflict over opinions, to resolve differences—these are the ways people in love heighten awareness and deepen understanding. The wedding itself is but a brief rite of passage; the engagement is the true period of transition from the single "me" to the married "us."

Somehow this realization all too easily gets lost in the many details of wedding planning. The wedding, not the loved one, is the focus of attention. Sadly, many couples find that, once engaged, they are actually spending less time together—and more of that time arguing about relatively unimportant things. Nerves get frazzled and relationships strained. The round of parties, the making of lists, and the shopping claim a disproportionate share of everyone's time and energy, and the whole reason for the ceremony becomes obscured.

The best way to combat this danger is by setting priorities and by vowing to communicate openly with each other and with everyone else who plays a part in your future life together. Marriage experts agree that a couple's ability to make decisions and to work out solutions to problems before marriage is a good indication of their ability to do so after. The engagement is where it all begins.

Communication with Each Other

To that end, ongoing communication with each other is essential. The engagement period can be a most exciting, revealing time for a couple. If you weren't shopping for your new home together, how else might you find out that his favorite color is puce? Who would have thought, before the visit to the caterer's, that crabmeat makes her break out in hives? All the seemingly endless routine tasks of wedding and marriage planning can become little inroads of discovery into the beautiful person you love.

"I have a real advantage here," laughs Al, thirty. "I know her so well, her good side and her bad, so I know exactly what I'm getting. I can really make a choice."

"I feel the same way," agrees Diane, twenty-eight. "After all this time, I don't think there's anything we haven't at least discussed. Sure, we've had our disagreements, our periods of uncertainty, but now we know that neither of us is perfect. We can choose to love in spite of what we know about each other—or maybe because of it."

Al and Diane have courted off and on for an unusually long time, six years, and are nearing the end of a six-month engagement. Over the years they have suffered through the death of Diane's mother, battled as Al started his own business, and drifted apart when graduate school consumed Diane's life. But through it all their honesty and their openness kept drawing them back together. "No matter how unsteady our love relationship got, we were always friends, we could always talk."

Communication: the art of speaking with and without words. It holds friendships together over time and distance. It enables them to grow and develop. It is the secret to lasting relationships, and its absence is the cause of those that break down.

Isn't marriage, after all, the ultimate friendship? Don't we expect our mate to be our friend and our nurse and our partner and our playmate and our lover as well as our spouse? Yet how can we expect so much if we have not taken the time or made the effort to discern how the other feels about these roles?

There is a prevalent misconception that good communication means letting it all hang out. Not so. There are some things better left unsaid, especially in times of anger and frustration. But good communication during the engagement period does mean a certain willingness to approach potentially discomforting subjects like sex or money, because sensitive subjects don't simply go away after marriage. Good communication depends on one's ability to listen to what *isn't* being said, to be in tune with nonverbal messages. And good communication depends on timing, particularly during the hectic pre-wedding days when so many other things vie for one's attention.

Food for Thought

In the interest of good communication, consider the statements in this list. Respond to them as honestly as you can, and ask your fiancé to do the same. Then compare and discuss your answers. You may discover some interesting, even surprising, things about each other. The discussion need not end with this list; we hope it will lead to close examination of the feelings and attitudes you each bring to the partnership.

1. I am comfortable with my partner's friends and family.
2. My partner respects my interests, talents, and opinions.
3. He/she brings out the best in me.
4. He/she is rarely jealous or overly possessive.
5. I am pleased with the ways in which my partner shows affection, and look forward to a satisfying sexual relationship.
6. We are able to talk about anything together: sex, money, politics, religion, etc.
7. My partner and I have been able to resolve conflicts and differences in a positive way.
8. I am pleased with my partner's career aspirations.
9. We are in agreement about the roles of husband/father and wife/mother in marriage.
10. I am aware of some of my partner's shortcomings.
11. I believe in personal loyalty and sexual fidelity.
12. We share similar views on childbearing and -rearing.
13. We are in agreement about our future lifestyle.
14. Getting married would make my life easier.
15. My family approves of my choice of partner.

Family Communication

While it is true that the wedding day belongs primarily to the bride and groom, they do not have sole proprietorship. In most societies, ours included, a wedding is an occasion of great joy and celebration. To deny those who love us participation in that celebration is selfish and inconsiderate.

Parents naturally experience a surge of excitement and sentiment when their son or daughter announces an engagement. A child's wedding, like his going off to school or renting his first apartment, is a landmark in life, a step into adulthood. It is a time of mixed emotions, of joy tinged with sadness. It is a time when families are keenly aware of their continuity from one generation to the next. It is a time to erase old hurts and anticipate new bonds.

In such an emotionally intense climate, good family communication deserves prime consideration from the engaged couple. We have already spoken of the impact families have on our lives, and the true force of this impact is often felt most during the period of wedding planning. For the couple, this period demands a unified front and adept shuttle diplomacy. The emergence of a new union and its future relations with the Old World depend on it.

The first step in family communication is for the couple to solidify that unified front. The two of you must agree, with common sense, good taste, and realistic limits, on the type, size, and style of wedding you want. Once that is agreed upon, you are ready to take your proposal to the families. If the families know each other and live within reasonable distance of each other, it would be nice to organize an informal get-together for the purpose of planning the wedding. If the families are not yet acquainted, this is the time to introduce them.

As is the case with most decisions of state, economics is a major matter for negotiation. Some families still prefer to assume the traditional breakdown of wedding expenses (see "Who Pays for What," page 64), but the escalation of wedding costs has precipitated a growing trend toward a more equitable sharing of expenses among the families and even the couple. Your prior knowledge of your own and your families' financial resources is your best guide to what to expect. But be prepared for some minor disagreements or misunderstandings—particularly if one family is more traditional about this sort of thing than the other.

The subject of money is always a point of contention, but common sense dictates that whoever is footing the bill has a right to a proportionate share of the decision making. If you and your fiancé are paying for the wedding and can afford whatever your hearts desire, then you can have a twenty-piece orchestra and a church full of orchids in December. If your parents are springing for a sit-down dinner for five hundred, then they just might expect a greater say in the guest list and dinner menu. If you insist on monogrammed guest soap in the ladies' room, then you buy it.

Whatever the breakdown of expenses, agree on a budget and stick to it. (See "The Modern Bride Budget Checklist," page 66.) Make sure everyone knows his or her financial responsibilities are and that he or she is comfortable carrying those responsibilities. And always remember that the details of a wedding are never more important than the feelings of the people involved.

Again, when families are similar in economic, social, religious, and ethnic backgrounds, this initial organizational task is much easier to accomplish. But when there are marked differences in lifestyle and tradition, a great deal of tact and understanding may be needed to keep everyone happy. A wedding is not the time to laud one family's wealth over another's, or to make either family feel disregarded or misunderstood. Obvious feelings of discord and discomfort will surely mar an otherwise lovely wedding day.

Sometimes bad feeling is generated unintentionally simply because the two families, who are probably not very well acquainted, do not understand each other's point of view. Here you and your fiancé can be a help by explaining matter-of-factly how the other side feels and by recommending a solution to their differences. Suppose, for example, the groom comes from an ethnic background in which a lavish feast is part of a wedding celebration, and the bride from one in which food is not considered an important part of the reception. Naturally, the bride's family may resent feeling pressured to provide a meal they do not feel to be necessary, and the groom's family may be disappointed by the entire reception if the catering seems too spartan. If the couple can suggest, without taking sides, a reasonable compromise—for instance, if the groom's family has the means, they might offer to pay some of the catering costs, or if it is an at-home wedding, to provide some homemade goodies—greater understanding and happiness all around may result.

Planning via long distance is another common hurdle many couples face these days. Here an extra effort is needed to help those far away feel more involved and important, and to clarify any misconceptions arising from regional differences in taste and style. (See "Special Considerations," page 154.)

Small problems and little misunderstandings are inevitable when so many people are involved in such a personal and stressful event. Many couples find that delegation of specific jobs to certain family members gives everyone a sense of belonging and helping. Decide who will do what, keep in touch with progress reports along the way, and treat every suggestion with appreciation, even if the suggestion is a bad one.

It is important to think of family participation in more than just monetary terms. Try to utilize talents and expertise to everyone's best advantage and fulfillment. Maybe your sister's personal taste rivals Liberace's, but she has his great ear for music. Take her along when you evaluate organists, and take someone else to help you put together your trousseau. Look for sensible ways to save yourself bother and to bring someone else pleasure. Perhaps your great aunt Nell, with time on her hands and beautiful penmanship, would be honored and delighted to address your invitations.

Small acknowledgments of family members' abilities not only relieve you of some of the burden of wedding planning but also provide a useful opportunity for them to show their love and support and to make a special contribution to your happiness. However, being polite and sensitive does not mean that you must universally accept every offer and defer to every wish. It is, after all, *your* wedding. If Uncle John, who is an amateur photographer, has volunteered to take the wedding pictures, but you would rather have a professional on the job, say so. Say it nicely, but say it. If you have organized carefully and thoughtfully, you have every right to reserve final judgment. The couple who cannot manage their wedding plans will have even more difficulty managing their married lives.

Communication with the Clergy

Since 75 percent of all marriages are religious ceremonies, it is not surprising that the clergy are increasingly sensitive to the conflict between the spiritual and material aspects of marriage planning. When asked what was the major problem he encountered with engaged couples, one priest commented, "They think more about the wedding than the marriage." In addition, several reported that people who never practice their faiths suddenly expect a big church wedding. They approach the cleric with a list of demands in much the same way as they approach a caterer. The whole focus is on the production; accordingly, the role of the minister, priest, or rabbi as religious celebrant and spiritual advisor is demeaned and dismissed.

Most clerics have a long history of family counseling, and many today are trained therapists. Their experience is valuable in matters of both God and man, and they should not be overlooked as a spiritual and practical resource. Communication with your cleric becomes a top engagement priority, especially if you are contemplating a religious ceremony.

Many faiths prescribe some sort of formal marriage preparation prior to the wedding ceremony. These preparations can range from mandatory prenuptial courses in many Roman Catholic dioceses to an informal chat with the cleric three weeks before the wedding. The style and extent of pre-marriage counseling is still usually determined by individual clerics and local custom, but a trend toward more structure is growing. In view of the high divorce rate, more and more clerics are considering prenuptial counseling to be an important aspect of their ministry.

The success of the Catholic model of the Engaged Encounter Weekend has spawned the Jewish Engaged Experience, the Episcopal Engaged Encounter, and the nondenominational Christian Tobit Weekend. Some Catholic parishes still require Pre-Cana Conferences, and many other denominations have devised similar workshops and seminars for their engaged couples. Rabbis typically meet with couples at least once to discuss the documents of marriage and the marriage procedure, but many of them are now expanding their premarital discussions into several sessions.

Not to be forgotten are individual waiting periods, legal paperwork, and specific marriage requirements in each denomination. Some are quite complicated, particularly when remarriage or differing faiths are involved. All in all, it pays to get to the cleric early in the engagement, not only out of respect for the spiritual nature of your commitment, but also because you probably can't set a wedding date with certainty until you do.

One final note on propriety. A cleric is best contacted by either you or your fiancé and seen by both of you together. If a great distance is involved, the officiant will usually make arrangements convenient for all. The point is, leave your mother at home. This is your marriage, and the two of you should communicate with the cleric so he can help you develop the kind of wedding ceremony you both want.

Becoming a Couple

The need for time together is particularly pressing during the engagement. That need must be met. You are emerging as a couple and your single friends and possessive families must be made to accept that. Don't allow your fiancé to be left out. Encourage engagement parties and showers that include you both. Set aside time for each other, time to gather your memories and to fashion your dreams.

Your togetherness must transcend both practicality and passion; it must extend into the realm of the future. Imagine your first Christmas or Chanukah together as husband and wife. Fantasize about your first anniversary. How might you celebrate it? Visualize what you see for yourselves in ten years. Where are you living? What kind of work are you doing? Do you have children?

Such daydreams are not just idle pursuits. They are manifestations of your expectations of marriage and projections of what you think married life might bring. The more dreams and goals you share, the more likely you are to fulfill them.

Finally, a fixed wedding date should not negate all the little niceties and flirtations of courtship. Indeed, the frivolities of a young romance should continue for a lifetime because love is nurtured through them. The greatest threat to any relationship is the complacency that comes with taking each other for granted.

As lovers and best friends, you will find thoughtful, romantic gestures particularly appreciated right now. Words that show caring or encouragement, cards or flowers for no special reason, unrequested favors and heartfelt thank-yous—each can bring you closer together and keep you mindful of your importance to each other.

Placed within the context of your future life together, the wedding day achieves its true significance. Whether large or small, opulent or simple, your wedding is a public profession of love and fidelity. It is not a Hollywood production. It is not a way to repay social obligations. It is not a vehicle for self-aggrandizement. It is in the end no better than the strength of your commitment. As such, it should reflect the dignity and solemnity of your marriage contract. Only then can your wedding day become the truly special occasion you want it to be.

Engagement Formalities

*D*o you realize how lucky you are to have made your own decision to marry? Centuries ago, when females were considered property and males were but necessary tools of procreation, marriages were arranged through heads of families or marriage brokers. Brides and grooms had little control over their fates, and love, like everything else, was a duty.

The custom of asking for the bride's hand in marriage evolved from this long tradition of male dominance and arranged weddings. The custom is still practiced in many cultures of the world, though rarely does a young man approach the prospective bride's father before she herself has agreed to the marriage.

Informing the Families

Contemporary American etiquette continues to advise couples to inform both sets of parents of the engaged couple before any public announcement is made. In some very traditional circles, a young man is still expected to have a private chat with the bride's father or parents. Since modern couples are older and more self-sufficient than they once were, these conventions are now more common courtesy than social necessity. However, many grooms want to make the gesture, whether expected or not.

Promptly informing the families also serves a practical purpose: it can alleviate, or at least minimize, future problems. Sometimes a prospective spouse is not exactly what a parent always pictured for his son or daughter. While it is unfortunate if your announcement has been met with a less than enthusiastic response from either of the families, you do not have to allow their initial reactions to undermine your decision. If you can be understanding of their feelings while maintaining a firm resolve, they may at least come to respect your right to marry whomever you choose.

Time has a way of calming misgivings for all concerned. The more surprising your news, the more time may be needed for others to accept it. This is particularly true for children. The prospect of a new stepparent raises immediate questions in a child's mind, questions ranging from "Where will we live?" to "Where do I fit in?" If either of you has children from a former marriage, those children deserve to be told first. Inform them alone or as a couple, but do it in a positive way and be evermindful of all youngsters' special concerns for love and stability when someone else enters their lives. (See "Second Marriage," page 188, for more discussion of this topic).

Setting the Date

Once the families have been informed, a wedding date must be set. This, too, involves consultation with the families, since the date must be convenient for all concerned.

January through March is the least active wedding season. If your preference falls into one of the more popular months, chances are that the availability of where you want to have the ceremony and reception will determine your exact wedding date and the length of your engagement. As previously mentioned, some religious faiths have required waiting periods. They may also forbid nuptials on special holy days or during certain liturgical seasons.

Trying to coordinate personal preference, availability, and religious requirements may sound a bit like the old "which comes first—the chicken or the egg" routine, but it can be done. Have a list of preferred dates and acceptable alternatives in hand before contacting the cleric. You may very well find that several dates are possible there, and then you can cross-check these openings with those at the reception site before making a final decision.

If yours is to be an informal civil ceremony in city hall, then reception reservations will be your only real concern. If, however, you wish to be married by a judge or any other particular state official, you had better contact him first.

Selecting Rings

Since Roman times, a plain gold ring has symbolized true and everlasting love. Worn on the third finger of the left hand, it was thought (falsely) that a vein ran

Remarriage and Children

We have all done a lot of kidding ourselves about the ease of re-marriage when children are involved. We think that because we love someone, our children will, too, or that because we don't have full custody of our children, they won't be an ever-present part of our lives. We have tried to eliminate the negative connotations of step family and stepparent by using words like blended, extended, or reconstituted. Most of all, because we see, hear, and read so much about the extended family, we become overly confident in our own ability to make it work.

But as Linda Bird Francke points out in her excellent book *Growing Up Divorced*, it takes more than eliminating a prefix to eliminate the difficulties of making one family out of two. Blurred parental roles, confused allegiances, and angry competition are more the norm than the exception, and the fact remains that divorce statistics are higher for second marriage than for first.

If you are contemplating marriage to someone with children or if you have children of your own, be realistic in your assessment of the situation. No matter how well you all may get along now, recognize that the children have probably not fully recovered from the impact of divorce, and that they may still harbor secret dreams of a reconciliation. The more time and energy demanded in resolving stepparent roles, the less time and energy you will have left to devote to your marriage.

The merging of stepsiblings, and eventual half siblings, adds yet another dimension to family difficulties. Your children will not necessarily like his, and in-laws will inevitably find it hard not to discriminate between blood relatives and inherited ones. All of these are very real issues that your love for each other may not be able to solve. You will have to confront the restrictions other obligations will set on your lives and face potential problems honestly. In complicated situations, premarital counseling might prove worthwhile.

directly from this finger to the heart. Today the ring may be considerably more embellished than a plain gold band, but the symbolism of the perfect circle remains.

Typically, the engagement ring is chosen with the wedding rings in mind, though this is not always the case. Nor is it necessary to have a diamond ring to signify an official engagement. Many women prefer other gems and stones to diamonds, or delight in the special significance of an heirloom from one of the families. Then there are those who forgo an engagement ring altogether in favor of using that money for a more elaborate wedding ring or some other wedding expense.

While some brides-to-be have no doubt been taken quite by surprise with the unexpected presentation of an engagement ring, it is probably safest to choose your rings together. The decision is facilitated by the professional advice of a reputable jeweler. Jewelry selection is a highly personal matter, and only a knowledgeable jeweler can explain the range of choices available within your budget. If you decide that a traditional diamond is for you, then you should be aware of the five Cs involved in determining its quality.

Cut refers to shape and to the skill and precision through which a rough diamond is transformed into a brilliant, faceted gemstone. The six most popular cuts for engagement rings are: round, oval, marquise, pear shape, emerald, and heart shape. Diamonds are the hardest substance known (only a diamond will scratch another diamond), but they do have a grain, much like wood. Only a highly skilled diamond cutter knows the exact direction of the grain, which is the key to the successful cutting and faceting that gives the diamond its unique brilliance.

Clarity refers to the absence of serious flaws or blemishes in the stone. Slight flaws in high-quality diamonds cannot be detected by the naked eye. A truly flawless diamond, viewed through ten times magnification, is a highly expensive rarity. Here is where your jeweler can guide you. Ask to see the diamond you're

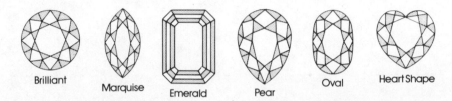

Brilliant   Marquise   Emerald   Pear   Oval   Heart Shape

Illus. 1.   Diamond Cuts

considering under magnification. Although serious flaws can affect the durability of the diamond, a stone with very slight flaws can be perfectly acceptable in your price range.

Color refers to body color, not to the surface that reflects light. It is sometimes difficult to distinguish between the actual color of the diamond and the sparkle you see coming from the facets, especially under artificial light. True colored diamonds are rare and expensive, but with conventional white diamonds, color refers to the degree of shading in the clear stone. A diamond with overtones of yellow is less valuable than a clear, colorless white one. Once again, let your jeweler be your guide.

Carat refers to the total weight of the stone. A carat is divided into a hundred points, so a ten-point diamond weighs one-tenth of a carat. Obviously, as the other Cs indicate, bigger is not always better; a small, nearly perfect gem can be a great deal more valuable than a larger, less perfect one.

Certification refers to a process developed by the International Gemological Institute that provides unquestionable proof of your diamond's identity and grade. Ask your jeweler for more information.

The first four Cs—cut, clarity, color, and carat—are the factors determining the price of your diamond. You will find a great deal of variation among them in your price range. If you covet a relatively large gem, you may prefer to sacrifice color and clarity in favor of size; conversely, if you would like a really fine stone, you will not choose the largest you can afford. Just make sure you understand exactly the quality and value of the gem you decide on.

Your jeweler should provide a written guarantee of the diamond's quality and characteristics, as well as permanent registration for the diamond you purchase. Obtain an appraisal and update it at least every five years. It is also wise to have your diamond ring professionally cleaned and checked once a year. Your jeweler has the equipment to revitalize your diamond's brilliance and the expertise to inspect the setting for subtle signs of loosening.

We might mention, too, that there are many lovely alternatives to the diamond engagement ring. Precious gems (sapphires, rubies, and emeralds) are available in a wide variety of beautiful sizes, shapes, and settings. Like diamonds, their price is determined by quality rather than by size alone, and their color, cut, and clarity will be important considerations. Often, precious gems are fashioned in combination with small diamonds or other gemstones, and the result is a truly impressive ring.

The semiprecious stones, such as opals, amethysts, garnets, topazes, and citrines, can also be set in stunning designs, and usually cost much less than diamonds or precious gems of the same size. If you are considering a semiprecious stone, however, do ask the jeweler about durability, and make sure the stone is free of internal fracture. Because most are rather fragile, the setting of a semiprecious stone is very important, and most jewelers will recommend that special precautions be taken with daily wear.

Not all retail jewelers will do custom design work, but many jewelery design studios specialize in original creations. They can rebuild or refashion antique jewelry, design settings for gems you may already own, or provide loose stones for your selection. Depending on what you request, their services are not necessarily any more expensive than any other jeweler's.

Make certain that you are dealing with a jeweler you respect, and be honest with him about what you like and what you can afford. An engagement ring is entirely a matter of personal taste and budget.

Your engagement ring should also be insured as soon as it is in your possession. If it is valued over a particular amount, usually $500, it should be included on a homeowner's or renter's household possession policy. Depending on its value, it may have to be listed separately on a personal property insurance schedule or rider at a nominal additional cost of so much per thousand. If you do not yet have your own household possession coverage, see about adding it to your parents' policy temporarily.

The ring from your fiancé is your first engagement gift, your first symbol of commitment. As such, it maintains a unique significance throughout your lifetime. While men don't wear engagement rings, many brides-to-be choose to commemorate this special occasion by reciprocating with a memorable gift of their own. A ring or other piece of jewelry or some other personal keepsake is a thoughtful acknowledgment of the bond between you.

Engagement Parties

Traditionally the bride's parents or sometimes the groom's parents host a party to officially announce the engagement of the couple. This, like so many wedding traditions, comes from the days when families were much more instrumental in the matching of young people. The successful match was therefore a cause for great family satisfaction and celebration.

Today engagement parties can take any form from an informal picnic to a formal cocktail buffet. Such an affair is essentially a welcoming gesture through which the prospective spouse is introduced to and accepted by the immediate relatives and close friends of the host family. Printed, handwritten, or telephoned invitations are acceptable, and guests are not expected to bring gifts because, supposedly, the engagement is not made known until the party.

More recently, this tradition has undergone some additional modifications. Now any one of a number of people might host the engagement party: a grandparent, a close friend, even the couple themselves when circumstances warrant. Sometimes, when the bride and groom are from different parts of the country and have met at college or at work, it may be necessary to have two engagement parties, one in each hometown. And sometimes, because of long engagements or complicated lifestyles, a couple may prefer to have no party at all.

"I'm sorry. I can't see it," snipped elderly Mrs. Oldguard over her afternoon tea. "I mean, the boy has been a fixture at family gatherings for as long as anyone can remember, so we certainly all know him. And I've been calling him and Joan engaged all along—for lack of a better word to describe their relationship. The whole family knows they live together, so who needs an engagement party?"

Mrs. Oldguard may sound straight and stuffy, but her point is worth noting. If a couple has been a fixture for many years, an engagement party might be superfluous. Older, more conservative friends and relatives, especially those with whom the couple is not particularly close, often have difficulty understanding or accepting the trends in modern courtship. Thus they are not sure what reaction is expected of them, and may view invitations to parties and showers as simply surreptitious requests for gifts.

The whole question of propriety and intimacy before marriage still poses great difficulties for many. Families often refuse to acknowledge that their young people are living together outside of marriage. Couples find themselves playing out a charade when they visit home. Such pretense all around makes people ill at ease, even resentful.

Mrs. Oldguard believes herself to be in a compromised position: she doesn't really approve of the couple's lifestyle, but she feels obligated to the family. If you have a more liberal philosophy on moral behavior, simply be aware that not everyone shares your view. Give that thought consideration when making your wedding plans.

As in any social situation, use good sense and good taste when deciding what kind of engagement party, if any, you will have. Include on your guest list only those who, through personal or professional association, have a reason to be there and to share in your happiness.

Both you and your fiancé must be in attendance, and people are generally not invited to an engagement party if they will not also be asked to the wedding (the exception is made when the wedding is to be a very small, private one). Informal invitations should read: first line—your parents' name (or his if they are hosts); second line—your name (or his); third line—"To meet John Doe (or Mary Smith)." Be sure to send a written note of thanks to your hosts afterward, and to acknowledge in writing any gifts you may have received from guests.

Newspaper Announcements

If you are having an engagement party, it should be held just before, just after, or on the day the announcement appears in the local newspaper. Ideally the announcement should be sent to your hometown paper and to his if he lives elsewhere. If the two of you live and work in yet another city, you may also wish the notice to appear there for professional reasons.

The announcement usually appears from six months to a year in advance of the wedding and reads something like this:

> Mr. and Mrs. Peter Proper announce the engagement of their daughter, Patty, to Mr. Paul Perfect, son of Dr. and Mrs. Plu Perfect of Prettytown. A December wedding is planned.

Notice that the city is included only when it is other than the one in which the paper is published. Note, too, that the form will differ when parents are divorced or deceased. The society editor of the paper can help you with the appropraite wording in such circumstances.

You can request an engagement form for submitting all the information from the society desk of the paper. Many local publications include the educational and professional histories of the couple as well as other pertinent information about family background. If a form is not available, study the announcement style used by the papers and tailor yours to fit. Type or print all information clearly and indicate the date you would like the announcement to appear. Allow plenty of time: if in doubt, call and check with the society editor about the deadline for copy. Place the name and phone numbers of someone qualified to contact for verification on the top left-hand corner of each page.

Some of the larger papers will run accompanying photos either with the engagement or the wedding announcement, but not both. Local custom dictates whether the photo should be just of you or of both of you. If you are including a photo with the engagement announcement, submit a good-quality eight-by-ten-inch black-and-white glossy for each newspaper. A typed or printed caption giving your name(s) and a photo credit should be taped to the back, and the envelope should be marked "Photo—Do Not Bend."

Brides and grooms who are professionals may also wish to announce their engagement in the personals column of their company newsletter, professional journal, or college alumni magazine. This is an appropriate way to share your news with colleagues, and an easy solution to the dilemma of personal life versus business life.

Finally, a word about the formally engraved or thermographed engagement announcements which you may have seen. The word is incorrect. If you wish someone to be informed of your engagement, write a personal note or make a telephone call. Unlike wedding announcements (see "Announcements," page 75), printed engagement announcements are impersonal, serve no real purpose, and smack of soliciting gifts.

Broken Engagements

The ring, the party, and the newspaper announcement comprise the engagement formalities. If for any reason the engagement should be broken at this point, the ring must be returned to your former fiancé and any engagement or wedding gifts received from friends and relatives thus far must be returned with a note stating that you have broken your engagement by mutual consent—even if it wasn't mutual. A similarly worded notification should also be sent to any newspapers that printed your engagement notice. The tragedy of death also necessitates the return of gifts and notification to papers, though a member of the bride's family usually assumes such duties for the bereaved party.

A broken engagement is unfortunate, but it does not make you a social outcast. You are not required to make any excuses or explanations beyond the simple statement of fact. The details of the decision are strictly between you and your former fiancé, and they should stay that way.

Wedding Preparations

While you are taking care of engagement formalities and beginning to plan your wedding, you'll want to give careful thought to the selection of your attendants. If your wedding is to be small (under fifty people), you'll need only a maid or matron of honor and a best man. The rule of thumb for a large wedding is one usher for every fifty guests.

Since it is nice (but not essential) to have an equal number of bridesmaids, you will want to discuss this matter with your fiancé when deciding on the type of wedding you will have. Practical considerations such as time, distance, and expense are involved. While it is indeed an honor to be asked to take part in a friend's wedding, it can also be a hardship. Talk honestly with those you select, and be understanding of their circumstances if they cannot participate.

Selection of Attendants

A bride and groom usually choose close friends or relatives for the honor positions. In recent years young men have asked their fathers to be best man. In cases of remarriage, parents may select a son or daughter. (Small children should be only ring bearers or flower girls, girls between nine and twelve can be junior bridesmaids, and adolescents are acceptable in any role.) These contemporary choices are lovely gestures indicating a friendship as well as a kinship.

Whomever you choose, your selection of attendants should be made from among those who have special places in your lives. They may be single or married, and the participation of one does not necessitate the participation of his or her spouse. At one time pregnant women were not considered appropriate choices, but that taboo has disappeared. All your attendants should be people who are truly interested in your happiness and who are willing to help you with the myriad details of wedding planning and organization. Neither of you is obligated to have relatives of the other in the wedding party unless you want to.

For a younger bride, the selection of attendants often becomes an awkward task, especially if she does not have ample family to fill the ranks. Announcement of bridesmaids is tantamount to a public listing of friends in descending order. If you are wrestling with this difficulty, here are some things to consider: generally, a friend of longer standing takes precedence over a newly acquired one; having been an attendant in another's wedding does not require you to reciprocate; the size of your wedding fixes limits on the number of attendants you have; and most friends have an innate sense of where they fit into your life. Be as diplomatic and gracious as possible, but ask only those you really want.

There are also some creative ways to include people dear to you but not appropriate for the wedding party. A younger cousin, for example, can distribute rice bags at the reception. A former roommate might preside at the bridal book. In many areas of the country, where receptions tend to be held at home or to be less of a professionally catered affair, older friends and relatives are designated as members of the house party. The women wear small corsages and have special responsibility for seeing that things go smoothly at the reception. With a little ingenuity, you too may be able to devise a method by which a special individual can have a unique role in your wedding celebration.

Compiling the Wedding Guest List

While we're on the subject of people, now is also the time to begin compiling the guest list. Interviews with brides and grooms indicate that this may be the most difficult task in wedding planning because it can so easily get away from you. Compiling a guest list demands a great deal of discipline and family communication.

The most common question is "Where do we draw the line?" The most common response is "It's gotten out of hand!" To avoid this desperation, let's preview the rules of the Guest List Game: (1) the size of the wedding is determined by your budget; (2) the guest list should be fairly evenly distributed between your friends and the friends of each of your families; (3) the size of your guest list has an influence on the style of your wedding; (4) you should not invite anyone to your wedding just to repay a social debt; and (5) ex-spouses are never invited to your wedding. (For more details, see the chapters on wedding styles and budget in Part Two.)

However, knowing the rules and applying them are two different things. Family traditions figure largely in determining the guest list. For many families a wedding is a time to bring all the relatives, however distant, together. Socially prominent families may seek to impress the community with a gala event. Families of professional people may look to deduct the wedding as a business expense. Who draws the line? You do. It's your wedding.

It's important to draw this line *before* you ask your parents and in-laws to draw up their lists. If you let them compile a list of a hundred people when you can only accommodate fifty, and then ask them to cut it by half, they'll come up with a million reasons why so-and-so just *has* to be invited. It's far easier to give them a firm limit of fifty to start with and make it clear that you expect them to be ruthless in weeding out the surplus.

It's up to you to be able to deal with your families and to adhere to the limits you have all agreed upon. If things do get a little out of control, keep in mind that not all those invited will ultimately attend. With luck you will be able to project the actual number of guests you will have.

Properly speaking, no one should be invited to the wedding who is not invited to the reception, though you may do it the other way around if you choose to have a very intimate wedding ceremony. Wedding announcements are sent to those whom you cannot accommodate.

Start early on your guest list, and start by compiling your own with your fiancé. That will give you an idea of just how much "family communicating" you have ahead of you.

Honeymoon Homework

One of the most pleasant engagement tasks is the planning of the honeymoon. Unless you are going to have an unusually long engagement period, preparations for the honeymoon should begin as soon as you set your wedding date. Popular destinations, like the Caribbean, Florida, the Poconos, Hawaii, or Mexico, get booked far in advance, especially during peak seasons.

As one travel industry executive advises: "I think a good travel agent is your best ally. Agents can book it all: they have instant information on availability, they enjoy a higher priority on waiting lists, and they will generally work harder to get you exactly what you want. Plus reputable agents are accustomed to working within budgets, and most have had lots of experience in honeymoon planning." In these days of deregulation and stiff competition for the travel dollar, it pays to shop and compare. A travel professional can help you do this efficiently while also being attuned to the many details of a trip that you haven't time to worry about.

The key to a successful honeymoon is finding a destination offering a balance between the activities you both enjoy and the privacy you both covet. This nat-

urally is as individual as your idea of fun or romance. Couples with athletic pro-
clivities might enjoy a ski lodge or a sports resort. More studious types might
choose an area with some history to explore. Whether you choose a cruise or a
campground, plan your honeymoon with intimacy and mutual interests in mind.

"It was the trip of a lifetime," said Joan after her return. "But we really had
our honeymoon when we got back. Fourteen European countries in twenty-one
days left us cross and exhausted. We felt guilty if we didn't see everything and
take every tour. What with all the trains and buses, the packing and unpacking,
we became more like roommates than lovers." Some couples who want the trip of
a lifetime choose to postpone their honeymoon until a few weeks or months after
the wedding. There is no law saying you have to leave on your honeymoon immediately after the reception. Alternatively, you might want to take a few days
right after the wedding in a relaxing nearby place to recuperate from the wedding
festivities, and save the big, elaborate honeymoon trip for later on. As with every
other wedding and marriage decision, choose the place and the time and the style
that suit the two of you.

Lifestyle Preparations

*T*he bridal gift registry has been successfully used by several generations of brides, but never has it been a more exciting or comprehensive service than it is today. If you're not familiar with this convenience, you should be.

Bridal gift registry is a free service offered by department and specialty stores that allows you to list the items you need and want for your new home. It is an easy, convenient way for guests to select gifts and for you and your fiancé to coordinate household furnishings without duplication and the bother of returns.

Gift registry obligates no one and is an efficient way for family and friends to be sure their gifts are appreciated. (They can even order gifts by phone.) It is particularly recommended when you're having a large wedding; your parents' friends, distant relatives, and others may not know anything about your tastes and lifestyle, and their most sincere attempts to please you can often result in white elephants. They'll be grateful for the guidance the bridal registry provides.

Using the Gift Registry

The ideal time to register is as soon as you announce your engagement. This way the registry is available for engagement and shower gifts as well as for wedding presents. You simply go to your favorite store, sit down with their bridal gift registrar, and fill out a selection form indicating what you do and don't want. (See the sample checklist on page 30). Then whenever one of your guests uses the service, he or she will be able to choose a gift from those you've indicated on your form. The gift is recorded so that no one else using the registry will duplicate the selection (except of course in flatware or china, where you hope to build complete sets).

Gift registrars are not only masters of coordination and organization but are also totally familiar with all the products and trends in the home furnishings market. They are generous with their time, helpful with their advice, and practical about designing a list to meet all price ranges for gift-giving. They will encourage you to take your time and think about your selections, so it's probably a good idea to do a little window shopping and magazine thumbing (in *Modern Bride*, of course) before sitting down with the consultant.

"Though several stores in my small hometown were offering bridal registry services when I got married, I really didn't understand what it was all about and never bothered to investigate it," admits Janet, who ironically went on to build a career in bridal gift registry with a major retailer. "The result was that most of my wedding gifts came in avocado green, a big color at the time, a color I never liked and am still stuck with fifteen years later."

Janet cautions young women against making her mistake. "Just because you register, it doesn't mean your family and friends *have* to select gifts from the registry. But by registering you are giving people a choice, freeing them from being forced to guess what you want. A lot of people will appreciate that, and you just might appreciate not having to run all over town exchanging things."

Making Your Selections

You can register whatever you wish wherever you wish. Obviously, larger stores have a wider range of merchandise from which to choose, but even smaller stores are moving away from just tabletop selections into more general household items for fuller coordination. You will find items that reflect whatever is current in your lives, from electronic gadgets to newly designed luggage.

Some of the larger chain stores have incredibly sophisticated, computerized cross-referencing systems that may allow you to be registered simultaneously in more than one location. Even those without computerization can keep records of your registration throughout branch stores. If you and your fiancé are from different areas of the country, you may want to consider a large store convenient for both sets of family and friends. (It is advisable, in any case, to register in both locations, even if at different stores.)

When you are registered with more than one retailer, you must be responsible for updating each registrar on gifts received. Also, if items that have been registered come from other sources, you must inform the registrar(s).

Modern Bride's Gift Registry Checklist

FORMAL DINNERWARE

Manufacturer:_____

Pattern:_____

	Quantity
Dinner plates	_____
Salad/dessert plates	_____
Bread/butter plates	_____
Soup bowls	_____
Fruit bowls	_____
Coffee cups/saucers	_____
Teacups/saucers	_____

	Quantity
Demitasse cups/saucers	_____
Coffee server	_____
Teapot	_____
Sugar bowl/creamer	_____
Vegetable dishes	_____
Covered casseroles	_____
Platters	_____
Serving bowls	_____
Gravy boat	_____
Salt/pepper shakers	_____

CASUAL DINNERWARE

Manufacturer:_____

Pattern:_____

	Quantity
Dinner plates	_____
Salad/dessert plates	_____
Bread/butter plates	_____
Soup/cereal bowls	_____
Fruit bowls	_____
Cups/saucers	_____

	Quantity
Sugar bowl/creamer	_____
Vegetable dishes	_____
Covered casseroles	_____
Platters	_____
Serving bowls	_____
Covered butter dish	_____
Mugs	_____
Gravy boat	_____
Salt/pepper shakers	_____

STERLING/SILVERPLATE FLATWARE

Manufacturer:_____

Pattern:_____

	Quantity		Quantity
Knives	_____	Serving spoons/fork	_____
Forks	_____	Cheese serving knife	_____
Salad forks	_____	Salad servers	_____
Soup spoons	_____	Gravy ladle	_____
Teaspoons	_____	Pie server	_____
Iced-beverage spoons	_____	Cake knife	_____
Demitasse spoons	_____	Pickle/lemon fork	_____
Butter spreaders	_____	Sugar spoon	_____
Butter serving knife	_____	Silver chest	_____
Pierced tablespoon	_____		

STAINLESS FLATWARE

Manufacturer: _____

Pattern: _____

	Quantity		Quantity
		Iced-beverage spoons	_____
		Butter spreaders	_____
Knives	_____	Butter serving knife	_____
Forks	_____	Pierced tablespoon	_____
Salad forks	_____	Serving spoons/fork	_____
Soup spoons	_____	Gravy ladle	_____
Teaspoons	_____	Cake/pie server	_____

SERVING ACCESSORIES

	Quantity		Quantity
Chafing dish	_____	Baskets	_____
Compote	_____	Well and tree platter	_____
Coffee/tea service	_____	Salad bowl	_____
Sugar bowl/creamer	_____	Salt/pepper shakers	_____
Serving trays	_____	Cheeseboard	_____
Serving cart	_____	Soup tureen	_____
Trivets	_____	Candlesticks	_____
Cake plate	_____		

FINE CRYSTAL

Manufacturer: _____   Quantity
Pattern: _____   Hoch wine   _____
                              Quantity   Cordials   _____
Goblets   _____   Brandy snifters   _____
Champagne/flutes   _____   Decanters   _____
Champagne/sherbets   _____   Pitchers   _____
Wines (red/white)   _____   Vases/bowls   _____

CASUAL GLASS/BARWARE

Manufacturer: _____   Quantity
Pattern: _____   Highball   _____
                              Quantity   Old-fashioned   _____
All-purpose wine   _____   Pilsner/beer glasses _____
Tumblers   _____   Iced beverage   _____
On-the-rocks   _____   Juice   _____

BAR EQUIPMENT

                    Manufacturer   Manufacturer
Ice bucket   _____   Champagne cooler _____
Wine cooler   _____   Punch bowl set   _____
Wine rack   _____   Cocktail shaker _____
Decanter   _____   Jiggers   _____
Carafe   _____   Coasters   _____
Pitcher   _____   Bar utensils   _____

COOKING EQUIPMENT   Manufacturer   Quantity

Saucepans   _____   _____
Sauce pot/bain-marie   _____   _____
Skillets   _____   _____
Covered casseroles   _____   _____
Omelet pan   _____   _____
Double boiler   _____   _____
Dutch oven   _____   _____

	Manufacturer	Quantity
Stockpot		
Microwave cookware		
Roaster and rack		
Wok		
Pie pans		
Cookie sheets		
Muffin tins		
Cake pans		
Lasagna pan		
Quiche dish		
Soufflé dish		
Fondue pot		

ELECTRICAL APPLIANCES

	Manufacturer	Model Number
Toaster oven		
Toaster		
Mixer		
Blender		
Food processor		
Coffee maker		
Coffee grinder		
Frying pan/skillet		
Waffle iron/griddle		
Can opener		
Electric knife/food slicer		
Warming tray		
Slow cooker/crockpot		
Corn popper		
Ice cream maker		
Espresso/cappuccino machine		
Pasta maker		
Juicer		
Steamer		
Wok		
Yogurt maker		
Rotisserie/broiler		
Microwave/convection oven		

KITCHENWARE

	Manufacturer		Manufacturer
Canister set	_____	Thermometer	_____
Cutlery	_____	Food scale	_____
Steak knives	_____	Eggbeater	_____
Cutting boards	_____	Can/bottle opener	_____
Cookbooks	_____	Measuring cups/spoons	_____
Teakettle	_____	Whisks	_____
Cookie jar	_____	Graters	_____
Utensil set	_____	Strainers	_____
Timer	_____	Vegetable peeler/corer	_____
Mixing bowls	_____	Baster	_____
Storage containers	_____	Molds	_____
Kitchen clock	_____	Colander	_____
Spice rack	_____	Ice cream scoop	_____
Pepper mill set	_____		

LINENS

Bedroom:	Size	Color	Quantity
Flat sheets	_____	_____	_____
Fitted sheets	_____	_____	_____
Pillowcases/shams	_____	_____	_____
Pillows	_____	_____	_____
Blanket, lightweight	_____	_____	_____
Blanket, woolen	_____	_____	_____
Electric blanket	_____	_____	_____
Bedspread	_____	_____	_____
Comforter/quilt	_____	_____	_____
Duvet	_____	_____	_____
Mattress pads/protectors	_____	_____	_____
Pillow protectors	_____	_____	_____

Kitchen:

	Size	Color	Quantity
Dish towels/cloths	_____	_____	_____
Pot holders/mitts	_____	_____	_____
Apron	_____	_____	_____

Bath:

	Size	Color	Quantity
Bath sheets			
Bath towels			
Hand towels			
Washcloths			
Guest towels			
Bath mat/rug			
Shower curtain			
Shower massager			
Electric toothbrush			
Scale			
Hamper			
Shelf unit			

Table:

Tablecloths			
Runners			
Napkins			
Place mats			
Napkin rings			

HOME ENTERTAINMENT/ ELECTRONICS

	Manufacturer	Model Number
Television		
Radio/clock radio		
Stereo components		
Cassette recorder		
Video cassette recorder		
Video games		
Home computer		
Calculator		
Camera/photo equipment		

HOME FURNISHINGS ACCESSORIES

	Manufacturer	Style Number
Miscellaneous furniture accessories		
Lamps		
Card table/chairs		
TV trays		
Hurricane lamps		
Decorative clocks		
Frames		
Magazine rack		
Breakfast tray		
Decorative pillows		

HOME CARE

	Manufacturer	Model Number
Vacuum cleaner		
Electrikbroom		
Iron/ironing board		
Smoke alarm		
Fireplace equipment		
Sewing machine		

LUGGAGE

	Manufacturer	Color	Quantity
Tote			
Duffle			
Garment bag			
Carry-on			
Pullman			

Let your close friends and relatives spread the word about your registration. You can note where you are registered on shower invitations, but *never* on wedding invitations.

When choosing lifelong investments, like sterling silver or fine china, be sure they are items you will continue to enjoy and to use for many, many years. Good design is timeless—and adaptable. It is no accident that certain manufacturers have been around for generations and that their names have become synonymous with the products they sell. In the major area of home furnishings, in those items that will receive extensive use or will be the focal points of your decorating scheme, buy the very best your budget will allow.

There is of course room for whimsy as well as practicality in your first home. But every choice, no matter how small, is a projection for the future, a prediction of the style of life you foresee for yourselves. The environment in which you live, the manner in which you entertain, the items you consider life's basic necessities are all indicative of your values and your personality. Try to be realistic in balancing your wants and needs. Why have a baroque silver coffee service if the only thing you're going to do with it is polish it?

Finally, the participation of the groom in this "shopping list for life" is the most important change gift registrars have noticed in recent years. One positive by-product of the sexual revolution is that men have become more involved in the style and quality of their home lives, and now feel as free to express themselves in the kitchen or in the nursery as in the boardroom. Even the man who may never have thought about it before will likely discover, when faced with a choice, that he prefers one pattern of bed linen to another. After all, he's going to be sleeping on it for a long time to come! Availing yourself of this service not only is fun but is another valuable way for you and your fiancé to communicate about your future lifestyle.

Wedding Showers

The bridal shower is a favorite engagement tradition and can take any form from a lunchtime celebration at the office to an elegant dinner at a private club. It is so called because traditionally the all-female guests shower the bride with gifts—usually useful items for her new home. Today, with many couples living on their own and an increase in second marriages, a shower may be given for both the bride and the groom as a couple.

If someone offers to give you a shower and you accept, you have certain responsibilities as the guest of honor. Do your best to accede to the type of shower your host wishes to give, to provide a guest list within the size range your host has indicated, and to supply the name(s) of the stores where you have registered your gift preferences. Make sure no one is invited to so many showers that it becomes a financial burden. Promptly acknowledge all gifts received with a thank-you note, and send a special note of thanks or a small gift to your host(s).

A shower usually takes place six weeks to one month before the wedding. It is given by a close friend, often a member of the wedding party. A shower should not be given by an immediate member of the bride's or groom's family because it seems as if the family is soliciting gifts. If a family member offers the use of a home and/or financial support, that person's name still does not appear on the invitation.

The main event at all showers is the bride's (or couple's) opening of the gifts. If you are beginning marriage with virtually nothing, a general shower is probably the best to have. If you are merging households and need to fill in items, a theme shower is the most practical. Choosing a theme adds to the fun and allows the guests to use their imagination and work within a budget. Discuss your needs honestly with your host so that the type of shower can be specified on the invitation.

Don't feel bound by tradition in choosing a theme for your shower. Anything that's useful or fun is appropriate. Californians Judy and Scott were feted with a Christmas shower shortly before their December wedding a few years ago. Each guest brought a tree ornament or some other carefully selected holiday decoration, and Judy and Scott have had the pleasure of recalling that special occasion and faraway friends each yuletide since.

Some other unique shower ideas include: a recipe shower, to which each guest brings his favorite recipe and one of the ingredients to stock the larder; a home-repair shower, in which each guest contributes a household tool or a piece of garden equipment; or a paper shower, for which guests bring stationery items or paper products for casual home entertaining. We've even heard of a shower by mail given for a bride whose fiancé, relatives, and friends lived all across the country and who would not therefore have had an opportunity for any pre-wedding parties. A theme was set by the organizer, and each "guest" was instructed to send a gift with a personal, humorous note about the situation. It may not have been a noisy, fun-filled gathering, but the warmth of intention was felt for miles!

No one should be invited to a wedding shower who will not also be invited to the wedding. There are of course exceptions to this rule: for example, when the wedding will be a family-only affair or when a shower is staged by co-workers and must necessarily include all those in a given department. In such cases, when you are not compiling the guest list, you need not feel uncomfortable about the distinction between personal friends and co-workers. You are, however, expected to acknowledge the gift(s), either individually or in a collective note.

For those of you who may want to follow the custom of displaying your shower and wedding gifts at home, here are some pointers: arrange gifts thoughtfully so that some don't pale by comparison to others; keep the display private, for family and friends, and avoid any public announcement of your display; and set up the display in an area of your home not heavily trafficked by casual visitors (delivery-men, etc.). Even if you decide not to have a formal gift display, you may still wish to share the excitement of special gifts with those close to you.

Topics for Premarital Discussion

After two decades of debate over the effects of environmental factors, peer pressure, and genes on human behavior, sociologists and psychologists are once again focusing their attention on the influence of the family unit. You need not study government statistics or peruse doctoral dissertations to know that the form and the function of families today differ from those of past generations. Whether or not you applaud the upheaval that has taken place, the reality of new social attitudes about the work ethic, sexual equality, children's rights, and individual freedom cannot be denied.

Marital Roles

Planning for marriage, then, involves much more than just comparing family backgrounds and getting to know each other as individuals. It also demands some honest soul-searching, some facing up to our deep-seated attitudes about roles and spheres of mutual responsibility.

"Since I had been married before, I told myself that I understood Andy's responsibilities to his first wife and their children," remarked Nancy, thirty-eight. "I was a liberated woman, I felt good about myself, and I was confident in my love for Andy and his for me. We were two mature people who had learned from our past mistakes and could face anything together." Now, surrounded by the toys and clutter of their own two-year-old son, Nancy appears anything but confident. She is exhausted from a summer-long visit with Andy's children, torn between continuing to stay at home with her baby or returning to her advertising career, dismayed by her jealousy over Andy's communication with his first wife, and embarrassed to admit that she is back in analysis again, asking some familiar questions about her role in life.

Betty Friedan, sociologist, feminist, and founder of the National Organization of Women (NOW), chose a thesis that surprised many for her book *The Second Stage*: "The new frontier where the issues of the second stage will be joined is, I believe, the family."[6] In spite of all the battles for equality won in the office, in the school, or in the legislature, the conflict between sexual roles and personal identity continues in the home.

It is relatively easy to be sure who you are and what you want when you are unencumbered—single. You set all your own priorities. Once you're married, however, you'll find that the needs and goals of others become intrinsic to the harmony and happiness of your own life. Thus when little Suzie comes down with a virus, your husband has an important sales meeting that day, and you are supposed to give a paper at the university in three hours, the best course of action is unclear because all the demands are equally important.

Your decision to marry reflects an awareness of the need for others in your life and an acceptance of the interdependency such a need creates. It will not always be easy to balance the different facets of your existence, but as Friedan points out, it is necessary to try:

> Personal choices . . . of women today are distorted when they deny
> the reality of both sets of needs: woman's need for power, identity,
> status and security through her own work or action in society . . .
> and the need for love and identity, status, security and generation
> through marriage, children, home, the family. . . . Both sets of
> needs are essential to women, and to the evolving human condition.[7]

Regardless of the gender roles that evolve in a marriage, remember that women *and* men are people first, with needs and feelings that override sexual stereotypes. The lasting marriage is an ongoing battle to protect personhood through care, compromise, conciliation, and even on occasion conflict. One gives when he or she is in the better position to do so, takes when he or she must. If you find yourself keeping score, then the battle is no longer worth fighting.

Whether the family consists of two members or ten, the good of the whole must be weighed every time the needs of members conflict. No one person's needs should ever have automatic priority. Every family, every situation, every day is different and requires a fresh approach to problem-solving and compromise.

"I'll make dinner, you clean up."

"You did the laundry, I'll fold it."

"I'm sorry, I just can't make it. You'll have to go without me."

"I could use some help with this."

"I know how you feel, but . . ."

This is the stuff of marriage, the everyday negotiations and decisions, the nitty-gritty of chores and trade-offs. No matter how well you think you know yourself, marriage will require new levels of maturity and an increased sense of selflessness and of self. You will find your roles by balancing your strengths and your weaknesses, and by meeting the demands of day-to-day living on a case-by-case basis. The proper roles for your marriage will not be easy to find; you will have to look for them.

Careers

Even now the subject of careers is so inextricably woven into the subject of sex roles that it is almost impossible to discuss one without at least touching on the other. Although feminism and economics have drawn greater numbers of women into the work force, most of us still feel stranded somewhere between the proverbial rock and a hard place. Women who witnessed creative, intelligent mothers being stifled at the kitchen stove are driven to be superwomen, while only the most self-assured men can truly be comfortable with the role of househusband.

The conflict of traditional roles—man as provider and woman as nurturer—with new social ideals and the growing necessity for two incomes has left us in a no-man's land of unresolved issues. What works for others may not necessarily work for us, so we as couples must reconcile our career aspirations with our role delineations on a more or less individual basis.

"What it came down to was that our endless discussions of what-ifs produced no real conclusions about how we were going to live," said Sarah, twenty-eight, after breaking her engagement. "I'm a professional woman, not a dilettante. I have a very real need to succeed in the world of finance. I don't know why, but that's not important. What is important is that I never led James to believe otherwise. He knew from the beginning that I was a workaholic, and I thought he understood that compulsion because he was one too."

James and Sarah are two dynamic individuals who met in college and were immediately drawn to each other. They both had career aspirations in New York and continued dating there after graduation. They both rose rapidly in their respective professions, and took an apartment together when it became clear that their schedules would allow them little time with each other if they didn't.

"I still love James," smiled Sarah. "I guess I always will. But that's not enough of a reason to marry him. I don't want a family. As the eldest of nine, I have raised enough kids already. I don't want to leave my job if he gets transferred. I don't want love to crumble into arguments—as it was already starting to do—over who does the dishes or who takes down the garbage. I guess I finally realized that we both needed a wife, and if we married each other, neither of us would have one."

The couple needs a wife—a common quip, that really isn't funny. If each of you isn't willing to be at least *half* a wife, to be the one who keeps the family running smoothly at least *half* the time, then you have no business getting married. Merely stating that your marriage comes first is as easy as saying "I love you," but really believing it when the going gets rough makes all the difference in both the quality and the duration of the union.

Dual-career couples with families *can* make it, but you must recognize the enormity of the struggle involved in making it work. In fact, sooner or later, for both partners, there will come a time when you will have to make sacrifices in your career for your family. If family isn't your ultimate priority, think long and hard about continuing your engagement. That takes a great deal of courage to admit, as Sarah did.

Financial and emotional satisfaction with your career yields strength and power. Whether that power is exerted in the international marketplace by corporate decisionmakers, or in the daily triumphs and achievements of the full-time homemaker, it is power nonetheless. Most of us are very protective of our own spheres of power, and conflicts inevitably result when those spheres are encroached upon.

A study of 6,000 American couples by University of Washington sociologists Philip Blumstein and Pepper Schwartz yielded some enlightening truths about the way we live and work as couples. Among other findings, they discovered that "no matter how large their paycheck, the working wives [60 percent of the total] were still almost entirely responsible for the couple's housework"; that most men detest housework, but most women, on the other hand, "even executives—did not consider housework demeaning"; and that, "because heterosexual men are unaccustomed to yielding power to women, they could take pleasure in their partner's success at work only if it did not challenge their own."[8]

The moral? Not that you shouldn't pursue a career with the same drive and commitment as your husband, but that you can't expect smooth sailing all the way. Try to assess in advance the trouble spots. Will it be getting him to share equally in housework? Try to plan an equitable arrangement now, and plan to adjust it often until the kinks are ironed out. Will it be his tendency to feel threatened instead of pleased by your professional accomplishments? Try to help him confront his feelings, and make him realize *your* success will never undermine *his* success or his value to you.

Although Blumstein and Schwartz published the results of their study as serious research in book form, they have been quoted as saying that they hoped people would "read it in bed" as a way to gain insight into their own lives. Not a bad idea. (See "Selected Bibliography," page 209.) When it comes to juggling careers and lifestyles and building our relationships, we need all the help we can get!

Financial Planning

People, and correspondingly families, are very strange about money. Some don't like to discuss it at all; others seem to talk of nothing else. Some see it as a means of achieving status and power; others dismiss it as one of life's pettier concerns. Some people hoard it, others give it away.

Regardless of individual attitudes, money is the tangible unit of compensation for goods and services in our society. Because of that, no one at any age should marry without the full disclosure of each partner's assets and liabilities. This does not suggest anything so ominous as a Dun and Bradstreet credit check, but it is a reminder that money is the most common cause of marital discord. Ignoring that fact won't make it go away.

The fact that brides and grooms are generally older these days means that often some premarital accrual has taken place. Many already own furnishings or a home, have insurance policies or profit sharing, pay alimony or child support. Prospective mates have the right to know all the assets and liabilities they will be assuming through their union with each other.

Even if you're starting out with a little between you, you still need to get your financial house in order to establish yourself as a couple. This is the time to consider wills, legal name changes, moving expenses, bank accounts, household management, credit cards, education loans, and anything else that may add to or detract from your solvency. (See Part III for more information.)

For younger couples, all of this should involve only a few hours of planning and discussion. For older couples, particularly those who have been married before or who have substantial holdings, a session with a lawyer or accountant may be helpful. Sometimes a premarital agreement or contract may be necessary or desirable. (See "Prenuptial Contracts and Agreements," page 192.)

Such overall fiscal planning will set the parameters of your financial lives together, but you will still have to work out the day-to-day manipulation of funds. It is in these matters that conflict often erupts. If money is power, then does the partner who has the larger personal income also have the larger say in how that income is spent? If money is to be enjoyed, then to what extent? What percentage of your income should be spent on entertainment or personal pleasures? Will you pool your resources and maintain a joint checking account, or will you keep your money separate in individual accounts?

Probably the best way to determine any potential trouble spots is by drawing up a preliminary household budget together. (See "The Household Budget," page 177.) Through the projection of income and expenses, a picture of each partner's financial contribution and responsibility will emerge. Then you can go from there to discuss priorities for discretionary funds. You will both be more comfortable if you know where you stand. Financial goals, like your other goals in life, should be clearly and unabashedly set.

Good financial management depends on spending less than is made. That way surplus funds are available for emergencies or extras. This is known as living within one's means, an amazingly new concept to a generation of credit card holders. Nonetheless, it is a highly desirable goal for a couple looking to assert itself and to achieve financial independence from families—and other lending institutions. (See "Your GMP," page 176.)

The more self-sufficient you can be as a couple, the more autonomy you will enjoy. You are becoming your own family now, in the eyes of both God and the IRS.

Family Planning

Most couples, even those who are eager to be parents, do not elect to have children right away. Thus, you will need to investigate the various methods of contraception available and decide which one you will use. (See "Guide to Contraception," page 46.) Personal health, religious values, and duration of use will all figure into your decision and, unless you are extremely knowledgeable about such matters, you'll probably want to seek the advice of a doctor or other health-care professional.

If you haven't already given this some thought, you'll want to do so at least six months before the wedding. Artificial methods such as the diaphragm or the pill require practice and/or implementation a couple of months before the wedding to be certain of their effectiveness; sympto-thermal charts and other "natural" methods demand a proficiency of technique that often takes several months to master.

Even if you are already sexually active and presumably using birth control, the period of your engagement is a good time to discuss any dissatisfactions you may both have with your current method and to choose a more satisfactory one. Start to use the new method before your honeymoon so that any unexpected complications with it won't ruin your special trip.

The question of parenthood should be addressed long before the wedding. Even though the woman bears the child, raising a family is something you do together and should be undertaken by mutual decision. Share your feelings about whether you would like to have children, and roughly when and how many. If you're both not sure whether you will want to raise a family someday, that's fine; you have plenty of time to decide. Just be sure you understand each other's feelings; nothing is more tragic than a marriage that goes sour because one partner expects to have children and the other doesn't.

Family planning is an intensely private and personal matter between you. Don't allow yourself to be intimidated by the opinions of friends and family members. Only by being open and honest with each other will the two of you be able to arrive at a decision with which you are both comfortable.

Guide to Contraception

HOW IT WORKS

The Pill

Chemicals similar to natural hormones prevent the ovary from releasing its monthly egg—no egg, no pregnancy. Usage: depends on packaging—most are daily for a month. Others may call for a pill a day for three weeks.

Intrauterine Devices (I.U.D.s)

Small plastic or copper-coated coils or other shapes placed in womb only by a physician. Affects womb lining so that it will not hold a fertilized egg.

New I.U.D. releases tiny quantities of hormone continuously for one year.

The following up-to-date information tells you what you need to know about the modern methods of contraception, so that you—with the advice of your doctor—can select the one best suited to you as a couple.

ADVANTAGES	DISADVANTAGES
99% effective when taken consistently and correctly.	Not safe for everyone—doctor's prescription needed.
No interference with your love-making.	Bad reactions in some—weight gain, hair loss, mood changes, nausea. Dangerous blood clots, heart disease, gall bladder problems, and hypertension in a small percentage of users.
Relief from painful periods for some women.	Low dose "mini pills" are safer but offer less safety from unwanted pregnancy.
	Pill can be forgotten.
Decision to use birth control made only once—thereafter the woman is always "ready" for sex.	2%–3% of users get pregnant each year.
Highly effective. Those with copper or hormones can be used by childless women.	Heavy periods and cramps, especially first few months. Less menstrual flow with hormone-releasing I.U.D.
	Tears of the womb and pelvic infections have been reported. Some doctors will not prescribe this for women who have not had children.
	I.U.D. may be expelled without knowledge. Hormone-releasing I.U.D.s must be replaced each year. Copper I.U.D. must be replaced every three years.

HOW IT WORKS

Diaphragm with Jelly or Cream

A rubber disc placed deep in the vagina in front of womb entrance. Must be used with spermicidal cream or jelly to prevent entry of sperm, and must be left in place 6–8 hours after intercourse.

A physician must fit the woman with the proper size diaphragm.

Foams, Creams

Spermicidal preparations are placed in the vagina to kill or immobilize sperm.

Foam is more effective than creams.

Sponge

Soft plastic soaked in spermicide. Blocks sperm entry. Spermicide inactivates remaining sperm.

Condom (or "Rubber")

Rubber sheath placed over penis to catch semen so it cannot enter vagina.

When used in combination with foam or other spermicidal barrier, there is added protection in cases of slippage or puncture.

ADVANTAGES	DISADVANTAGES
Completely safe. Highly effective.	3% of users become pregnant each year. Periodic need for refitting, especially after weight loss or gain of fifteen pounds. Lovemaking must be interrupted for insertion unless woman inserts routinely every night.
Prescription not needed. No physiological side effects.	Risk of failure often results from improper use rather than from product inadequacy. Requires interruption of love making to apply before each act of intercourse. May cause mild irritation in some women.
Prescription not needed. One size fits all. Safe. Effective for repeated intercourse within a 24-hour period without additional cream, jelly, or foam. As effective as foams, creams, and vaginal inserts.	Can be inserted only once. During intercourse it may slip to one side of the cervix. Could be costly if used as a frequent form of birth control.
90%–95% effective when used correctly. Completely safe. Doctor's help not needed. Prevents transmission of infections.	May interfere with lovemaking. Must be put on before any insertion; may detract from man's sensations. Occasional failures due to breakage, or incorrect removal of penis from vagina. It should be removed immediately to avoid spillage once penis becomes flaccid.

HOW IT WORKS

Vaginal Inserts (or Suppositories)	Small inserts containing spermicide dissolve in the vagina to form both a physical and chemical barrier to prevent sperm from impregnating.
Rhythm and "Natural" Family Planning	Refraining from intercourse on days when pregnancy can occur: for women with regular 28-day menstrual cycles, no intercourse on days 8 to 18 counting the first day of menstrual bleeding as Day 1. "Natural" family planning teaches women to identify secretions from the cervix, signaling days when pregnancy can occur.
Sterilization	Male: cutting and tying off the tubes within the man's scrotal sac that deliver sperm to the man's semen. Performed in the doctor's office under local anesthesia. Simpler procedure than in female. Intercourse is same as before. The male still ejaculates but there are no sperm in the ejaculate. Important: man must return to physician for follow-up examination to be certain ejaculate is sterile. Female: cutting and tying off the woman's fallopian tubes so that egg and sperm can't meet. Historically, done in the hospital and under general anesthesia. Laparoscopy is a newer, simpler procedure.

ADVANTAGES	DISADVANTAGES
Prescription not needed.	Effectiveness rates vary with different brands.
Effective when used consistently and correctly.	Need to wait between 5–15 minutes after insertion before each act of inter-
No applicators to insert, nothing to fill, clean, or remove after inter-	course, depending upon the brand.
course.	Effervescing suppositories may rarely cause minor irritation in either partner.
No physiological side effects.	
Acceptable to Catholic Church.	Very unreliable because day of ovula-
Will reduce considerably chances of becoming pregnant.	tion, when an egg is released and woman can become pregnant, may vary each month. Also, couples often yield to desire on unsafe days.
	Requires taking time to identify safe (nonfertile) days, but has been quite successful when conscientiously under-
	taken.
99% effective (in the rarest of cases ends of the tube somehow reunite).	Good only for couples who have had all their children or who should not have any for medical or other reasons—op-
Permanent—once man is assured his semen is free of sperm.	eration is usually irreversible.
Safe—usually no medical side ef-	Good only for women who are certain they will not want to become pregnant
fects, minor if they do occur.	in the future.
Virtually 100% effective.	
Permanent.	

Part Two
Your Wedding

Wedding Diplomacy

I sometimes think that the saving grace of America lies in the fact that the overwhelming majority of Americans are possessed of two great qualities—a sense of humor and a sense of proportion.

—FRANKLIN DELANO ROOSEVELT

*A*t first glance, it might seem odd that a statement from a politician is used to introduce the subject of your wedding. Yet in many ways a wedding is a very political event, involving knowledge, decision making, and diplomacy. Little wonder that throughout history marriages between governing families of different nations have always been arranged. What better way to ensure peace and solidify relationships?

Your wedding will probably not determine the fate of nations, but it will certainly be a pivotal event in your own history. As such, it is worthy of all the dignity and statesmanship you can muster, and some of Mr. Roosevelt's respect for a sense of humor and of proportion may be the saving grace in pulling it off.

Because a wedding is such an important event, and because the emotions surrounding it run high, people may place undue emphasis on relatively insignificant matters. All take themselves and their roles extremely seriously, and tend to waste energies better spent elsewhere.

As the bride, you must dispel the dangerous atmosphere of self-importance and pettiness. You must keep your priorities intact and maintain a lighthearted attitude about the little mishaps and mix-ups that undoubtedly will occur along the way. Will anyone even notice that one attendant's shoes are just a shade off color? Will the congregation be devastated if you stumble over a line in your vows? A beautiful wedding is a happy wedding where everyone, taking his or her cue from you, is too relaxed and joyful to care at all about the inevitable tiny snafus.

The wedding day belongs to the bride and groom. Your guests are there to enjoy themselves and to celebrate your happiness, not to pass judgment on the intricacies of the arrangements. It is your responsibility to take charge, to plan as thoughtfully and as thoroughly as possible, and to make sure everyone knows what is expected of him or her. Beyond that, there's nothing else you can do. Endless worry won't accomplish a thing—except perhaps add a few lines to your face before the wedding. And you certainly don't want that!

The Groom

Of course there may be problems you can't ignore involved with planning the wedding, not the least of which may be the groom. A man often feels left out because a wedding is something his fiancée may have planned in her dreams for quite some time. Meanwhile, he is only just beginning to cope with the reality that *he* is getting *married*. He's especially likely to feel this way if he is uncomfortable with the size or style of the wedding. Oddly enough, often the more macho, dominant men are the most susceptible to feeling left out. If they haven't taken an active part in wedding selections, considering such things as music and flowers to be women's concerns, then they will not feel as much a part of the event.

Ideally, the type and style of the wedding should reflect you as a couple. Yet in spite of the sexual revolution, the fact remains that most women are a great deal more adept at and more interested in social affairs than men are. You may have to be particularly sensitive to your fiancé's feelings about this "command performance," and especially mindful of his need to belong.

The best way to avoid friction between you is to keep the emphasis where it belongs—on the marriage. But do take steps to get him involved in the wedding, too. Perhaps he can take charge of some of the items he's more accustomed to handling, such as transportation, male attendants' attire, photography, and the honeymoon reservations. Ask his advice about your arena too—maybe he thinks the bridesmaids will look prettier in pink than peach, or he doesn't care for the idea of gladioli in the church, or he would love to see smoked turkey on the menu. There's more than enough to do to keep everyone busy and involved, so don't be selfish about letting your fiancé take the responsibility for whatever interests him, and take his opinions seriously when they're offered. Remember, it's his wedding too.

Relatives

For many of the same reasons, future in-laws are often a source of conflict. Unless thay are unusually close to you and your family, traditional bridal prerogatives may leave them feeling alienated. Typically, the bride's mother has first choice of wedding attire. The bride's parents are considered the hosts of the wedding, and the wedding itself is most often held on the bride's home turf. Moreover, if the bride's family is paying for everything, the groom's family will certainly be reluctant to voice opinions or raise objections to any of the wedding arrangements.

While things are changing somewhat, the traditional social and financial conventions of a wedding continue to deemphasize the role of the groom's parents. They reinforce the unfortunate sentiment of an old adage: "A son is a son till he takes a wife; a daughter is a daughter the rest of her life." Don't let that become the case for you.

Use the wedding to begin the integration of two families, recognizing the importance of each in your lives. Again, let your fiancé's parents be responsible for whatever they can: an engagement party, the rehearsal dinner, a social evening for the two families. Keep your future mother-in-law informed and give her some things to do, if she'd like. Bear in mind that without her you wouldn't have the man you love.

While we're speaking frankly, let's also admit that it is often not our future in-laws but our own families who create real conflicts. If you and your mother have never agreed on anything before, a wedding certainly won't alter that. It may be unfortunate, but just wishing it were otherwise won't make it so.

Even the best family relationships sometimes wear thin during the planning of a wedding. Lest you have forgotten, you are in charge. Give everyone a job to do, and ask for opinions *only* when you really might take the advice. Don't be afraid to stand firm on any decisions you and your fiancé have made, but don't be above deferring to someone else when that person is obviously right.

With the proliferation of extended families, you may find some situations to be particularly awkward. The roles of stepparents or stepbrothers and -sisters must be determined very carefully. Some extended families have congenial relationships; others do not. You may have to do some creative thinking to keep your wedding from being turned into a battleground for family feuds.

Twenty-one-year-old Laura lives with her father and stepmother, and she has a loving relationship with both. Her father and his family do not have a very pleasant relationship with her natural mother and her mother's large family. Laura, who loves them all, wants them all to share in her happiness. "Ever since I was a little girl," she says, "I've dreamed of a beautiful wedding with all the people I love. But now, after all that's happened over the years, I know that can't be. It would be disastrous to throw them all together, knowing they don't get along."

Luckily for Laura, everyone cared for her feelings. Through her, both sides of the family found a way to contribute to her happiness without hostility. The solution? Laura's natural mother gave a huge formal engagement party with her side of the family. Then her father and stepmother hosted a small formal wedding that included his side of the family. "Both events were lovely," said Laura afterward. "Even though I didn't have all the families together at once, I knew they all cared and were all with me."

Laura exhibited an unusual maturity and understanding for her age. She could differentiate between dreams and realities and was wise enough to effect a compromise in what seemed to be an impossible situation.

In every case you are the best judge of your families, of how they feel and what they are capable of handling. You can hardly expect to change long-standing patterns of behavior overnight. But you can capitalize on everyone's best intentions, even if you have to be a bit unconventional in implementing appropriate solutions.

Personal Anxiety

Finally, in anticipating problems, don't be alarmed if you start to experience some strange sensations yourself. Butterflies, sweaty palms, sleepless nights, moments of doubt and panic—all are manifestations of normal pre-wedding jitters. Getting married is a major step in life, and no matter how positive one is intellectually, there are bound to be some emotional rumblings. The groom may very well have them too. Such feelings aren't disloyal or foolish. They reflect the seriousness of the promise you are making to each other. Talking about your nervousness together, even laughing about it, may help.

How do you differentiate between normal jitters and serious doubt? You look to see if there are valid underlying causes for your fears. You take note of whether your doubts are fleeting or persistent. You go back and reread Part I of this book.

Wedding Styles

*T*o a great extent, the style of your wedding is determined by the size of the guest list, the overall wedding budget, the time of day, and the gown you choose. These specific considerations, within the framework of your own preferences as a couple, will guide you in selecting the style of wedding appropriate for you. Below is a brief description of the most popular styles.

Classic Formal

The classic formal wedding is steeped in tradition, dignity, and propriety. Because it is the most elaborate, it is usually also the most expensive. It presumes a sizable guest list (three hundred or more), employs every wedding protocol, and demands formal attire for the entire wedding party, even the guests, depending on the time of day and the social circumstances (diplomatic, political, or extremely affluent circles).

The bride wears a formal, traditional gown with a full veil or mantilla and a chapel-length or longer train. Since there are at least three hundred guests, there are a minimum of six groomsmen (one for every fifty guests)—probably more—and an equal number of bridesmaids. In addition, the wedding party may include a flower girl or two, a ring bearer, perhaps even a train bearer, all outfitted in appropriate attire.

The classic formal wedding may take place in the late morning, the late afternoon, or the evening, and is followed by a formal reception and a sit-down luncheon or dinner. Obviously, the ceremony and reception should be held in impressive locations that can accommodate all the guests invited to both places. (St. Patrick's Cathedral or Westminster Abbey would be nice!) Invitations should be engraved with the traditional wording and would not include reply cards. At such a large wedding, seating sections are often reserved for family and special friends. Pew cards for this purpose would be included with the invitations.

There are those whose social position or international reputations demand the classic formal wedding. But even they would admit that the protocol of such an affair is staggering and necessitates months of planning by professionals. For most people, such an elaborate production is not possible or even desirable.

Formal

The formal wedding is what we usually envision when we think of a traditional wedding with all the trimmings. It generally involves between a hundred and two hundred and fifty guests, with three to six bridesmaids and one usher for every fifty guests. There may also be a flower girl and a ring bearer. The bride chooses a long wedding dress and veil, and bridesmaids are in floor-length gowns as well. Guests wear dressy attire but are not necessarily expected in formalwear.

The formal wedding often centers on a religious ceremony followed by a formal reception. Invitations may be engraved or thermographed and may include reply cards. The wedding can be held at any time of day, and the reception fare, whether luncheon, dinner, or cocktail buffet, should be appropriate to the hour. Again, locations should be suitable to the degree of formality and the size of the guest list. If the place where the ceremony is being held is too small for everyone, you may invite additional people just to the reception. The situation may also be reversed. In both instances, two sets of invitations must be ordered and sent.

As with the classic formal wedding, the emphasis here is on tradition. Yet the rules of etiquette for a formal wedding are not quite so rigid and, therefore, allow for a broader interpretation to fit individual circumstances. For this reason, the formal wedding is a popular choice.

Semiformal

The semiformal wedding is smaller and less traditional than the formal wedding. The bride may choose a long or short gown of any color, and a matching hat, headpiece, or floral wreath rather than a veil. There are only one or two attendants, and they dress in keeping with the less formal choice of the bride. Guests usually number between fifty and a hundred.

Invitations to the semiformal wedding may be thermographed or printed by a photo-offset process. While the mood captures some elements of tradition, this type of wedding allows for a more individualized form and a more intimate atmosphere. It may be held at any time of day, and the reception often takes place at home *or* in a restaurant or club.

Informal

The informal wedding may be informal, but that is not to be confused with spur of the moment. Usually it is small, under fifty guests, involving only relatives and close friends, and is a civil, chapel, or at-home ceremony. Invitations may be printed, handwritten, or telephoned. The bride chooses a street-length dress or suit, and others dress accordingly. Only a best man and a maid or matron of honor attend the couple, and the reception may consist of refreshments at home or dinner out.

The dominant element of the informal wedding is the intimate sharing of an important occasion in the lives of the couple. It is simple and relatively inexpensive, but just as important and memorable as the most lavish wedding.

Whatever kind of wedding you choose, let it reflect your couplehood. The measure of a beautiful wedding is not how much it costs but how much it reflects what's most important to you both. Your happiness at this time projects an aura that makes the difference.

Dollars and Sense

*F*act: The bridal market is a $17 billion a year industry. Conclusion: Weddings cost money.

The average wedding in America, including all related goods and services, runs between $5,000 and $6,000. Obviously, some people spend a great deal more, while others spend much less. It takes no financial wizardry to understand that if your funds are virtually unlimited, you can have whatever size and type of wedding you want; conversely, if money is tight, then some choices and compromises will have to be made.

For most of us, funds *are* more or less limited, and a wedding budget is vitally important. Today it is essential to be a knowledgeable consumer in order to get the most for your dollars. A budget provides guidelines. From these, priorities are established and comparison shopping follows. No one should have to go into debt to achieve a beautiful wedding.

As already discussed in Part I, the first step in taking charge of wedding plans is for you, your fiancé, and your families to determine what kind of wedding you will have and who will pay for it. Be honest and realistic in these discussions; to do otherwise is to court discord, disappointment, and debt.

Basically, there are four ways wedding costs can be handled: (1) in the traditional manner, with the bride's family shouldering the bulk of the expense (see "Who Pays for What," page 64); (2) the bride's family and the groom's family divide the total wedding cost; (3) the couple assumes some of the expenses along with the families; or (4) the couple pays for everything. In addition, it is not unheard of or improper for the groom's family to assume almost total financial responsibility for the wedding. (For invitations under such circumstances, see page 73.) A benevolent relative—an aunt, uncle, or grandparent—may also offer some specific wedding contribution as a special gift to the couple.

Today, there simply is no right or wrong way to distribute the expenses of a wedding. They are often distributed on the basis of one's willingness and ability to pay. Just be sure that everyone involved agrees on the budget and that all know exactly what their financial responsibilities are. Once the agreements are made, it is up to you to make sure that financial limits are respected.

Budgeting Your Wedding

To get you started, let's use the formal $6,000 wedding as an example and list approximate percentages of the total budget spent for major items:

Invitations and stationery	4%	$ 240
Attire	12%	720
Flowers	7%	420
Photography	8%	480
Music	9%	540
Reception	50%	3,000
Miscellaneous (gifts, favors, fees, transportation, etc.)	6%	360
Unexpected (taxes, tips, etc.)	4%	240
	100%	$6,000

(Note that this does not include rings, attendants' or mothers' attire, or honeymoon expenses.)

While this is an approximation of how expenses are distributed, nothing says yours must be this way. Often it is not, because a great deal of the wedding expense depends on the size and type of wedding you're having, the area of the country in which you live, and the local wedding customs of your community. If, for instance, your reception will consist of wedding cake and sparkling wine or punch in the church hall, then you will hardly need to allot 50 percent of your total budget to cover that. But if you plan a formal sit-down dinner at a popular hotel or caterer in a major city, then you will probably have to allot even more than 50 percent of the budget for the reception.

64

Who Pays for What

There aren't absolute rules on who pays for what. Traditionally the wedding expenses have been borne primarily by the bride's family, with the groom responsible for the rings and honeymoon. While tradition is still an honored part of our heritage, financial obligations must often give way to everyday realities and compromise. The following list indicates the traditional assumption of expenses. However, the most important factor in deciding who pays for what in a wedding should be who is most willing and able to pay.

THE BRIDE

1. Wedding ring for the groom (if it's a double ring ceremony).
2. A wedding gift for the groom.
3. Presents for the bridal attendants.
4. Personal stationery.
5. Accommodations for her out-of-town attendants.
6. Physical examination and blood test.

THE GROOM

1. The bride's rings.
2. Wedding gift for the bride.
3. The marriage license.
4. Gifts for best man and ushers.
5. Flowers: Bride's bouquet and going-away corsage; corsages for mothers; boutonnieres for the men in the wedding party.
6. Accommodations for out-of-town ushers or best man.
7. His blood test.
8. Gloves, ties, or ascots for the men in the wedding party.
9. Fee for the cleric.
10. The honeymoon.
11. Optional: Bachelor dinner.

THE BRIDE'S FAMILY

1. The entire cost of the reception: rental of hall, if the reception is not held at home; caterer; food (including wedding cake); beverages; gratuities for the bartenders and waiters; decorations; music; flowers.
2. A wedding gift for the newlyweds.
3. The bride's wedding attire and her trousseau.
4. The wedding invitations, announcements, and mailing costs.
5. The fee for engagement and wedding photographs.
6. Ceremony: rental of sanctuary; fees for organist, soloist, or choir, and sexton (often included in charge for premises, but if this is free, these people have set fees); aisle carpets and/or canopy; and any other additional costs for decorations.
7. Bridesmaids' bouquets.
8. Gratuities to policemen directing traffic and/or parking.
9. Transportation for bridal party from the bride's house to the wedding ceremony and from the ceremony to the reception.
10. Bridesmaids' luncheon.
11. Optional: Rehearsal dinner.
12. Optional: Household furnishings for bride and groom from linens, china, silver flatware, and crystal to furniture.

THE GROOM'S FAMILY

1. Clothes for the wedding.
2. Any traveling expenses and hotel bills they incur.
3. Wedding gift for bride and groom.
4. Optional: The rehearsal dinner or other expenses they elect to assume.

THE ATTENDANTS

1. Their wedding clothes.
2. Any traveling expenses they incur.
3. Wedding gift for the couple.

THE GUESTS

1. Any traveling expenses and hotel bills for themselves.
2. Wedding gift for the couple.

Modern Bride's Budget Checklist

	Estimated Cost		Estimated Cost
RINGS		**PHOTOGRAPHY**	
Budget $_____	_____	Budget $_____	
		Formal portraits	
		Engagement	_____
STATIONERY		*Wedding*	_____
Budget $_____		Wedding album	_____
Invitations	_____	Parents' albums	_____
Announcements	_____	Extra prints	_____
Thank-you notes	_____	Video recording	_____
Reply cards	_____		
Other *(maps,*		**WEDDING PARTIES**	
at-home, pew)	_____	Budget $_____	
		Bridal luncheon	_____
		Rehearsal dinner	_____
FLOWERS		Out-of-town guests	_____
Budget $_____			
At wedding site	_____	**RECEPTION**	
Bridal bouquet	_____	Budget $_____	
Attendants'			
(male, female)	_____	Food	_____
Mothers' corsages	_____	Beverages	_____
At reception site		Wedding cake	_____
(centerpieces,		Gratuities and taxes	_____
head table, backdrop)	_____	Escalation clause	_____

	Estimated Cost		Estimated Cost
MUSIC **Budget $_____**		**FEES** **Budget $_____**	
Wedding	_____	Church/synagogue/ other site	_____
Reception	_____	Officiant	_____
		Assistants (cantors, altar boys)	_____
BRIDAL OUTFITTING **Budget $_____**		Bridal consultant	_____

Dress	_____	Attendants (parking,
		  ladies' room,
		  police officers, etc.)
			_____

Headpiece and veil	_____		
Undergarments	_____		
Accessories	_____		
Hairdresser	_____	**EXTRAS**	
Trousseau	_____	**Budget $_____**	
WEDDING ATTIRE **Budget $_____**		Monogrammed napkins	_____
		Matches	_____
Groom's outfit	_____	Guest towels	_____

Attendants' apparel
  (male and female)
	_____	Favors, groom's cake
		  and boxes
			_____

Mothers' attire	_____	Rice bags, garter	_____
		Hotel accommodations	_____
GIFTS **Budget $_____**		**HONEYMOON** **Budget $_____**	
Bridesmaids	_____		
Groomsmen	_____	Transportation	_____
Other	_____	Accommodations	_____
		Daily allowance	_____
TRANSPORTATION **Budget $_____**		**TOTAL BUDGET**	$_____
Limousines	_____	**TOTAL** **ESTIMATED COST**	$_____
Parking	_____		

Every budget necessitates choice. What you don't spend in one area can be spent on something else. Think about cutting back rather than eliminating, and look for ways to get the same effect for less money. Do your guests really need to dance to a twenty-five-piece orchestra, or will a five-piece combo do just as nicely? Might not the food be just as delicious and the reception just as elegant if arranged over brunch or lunch rather than dinner? Can you live with flowers which are in season rather than those which must be flown in? Or with a single blossom instead of a bouquet for yourself and your attendants?

Never scrimp on quality or taste. But you can certainly limit quantity and make economical choices between two perfectly acceptable alternatives. Beware of bargains that sound too good to be true (they probably are), and politely refuse offers from amateurs of dubious talent. On the other hand, if Uncle Milo is a well-known hotel pastry chef and he offers to make your wedding cake as his gift, then by all means let him!

While you're budgeting, don't forget to expect the unexpected. (Notice our sample budget.) Prices can go up, especially if you're talking about a wedding a year or more away. This should be specified in all your contracts. And surprises do happen, like cousin Florence, who never dates, showing up with an uninvited escort.

Also recognize that certain circumstances may severely limit your choices. The wedding put together in three months will undoubtedly cost more and allow for fewer options than the same kind of wedding for which there is plenty of time to comparison shop and plan. The size of the guest list and the expectations of the families regarding the amount of food and drink may mean that little extra niceties you would like must be eliminated unless you can pay for them yourselves.

Whatever your limitations, monetary or otherwise, look at your wedding planning as a challenge—the first of many that the two of you will face together over the years. Use the "*Modern Bride* Budget Checklist" on pages 66–67 and start right now to make time and money help you achieve the wedding you *both* want.

Inviting Your Guests

*P*erhaps no other single aspect of wedding planning is more troublesome than compiling the guest list. Just when you think you've got it all set, somebody remembers Aunt Esther or decides that Cousin Alvin can't possibly be excluded (and don't forget his wife and six kids). We have already previewed the rules of the Guest List Game in Part I (page 25), but one point is worth repeating: you and your fiancé should draw the line on size *before* you ask the families for their lists, and every effort should be made to invite all guests to both the wedding and the reception. That reiterated, let's go on to specifics.

A generation ago, the total number of guests was usually divided in half between the two families, no matter who was paying. Today, since the bride and groom are usually older with friends of their own, it probably makes more sense to divide the guest list into thirds: a third for each family and a third for the couple. It is then up to each of the parties to figure out workable methods of limiting their portion of the list.

Some *very* large families draw the line at first or second cousins. Other families may eliminate all business associates, considering the wedding to be more a private affair for friends and relatives. Sometimes it may be decided not to include escorts of single guests. Such cutoffs sound harsh, but they are often the only way to impose limits. Wedding invitations should never be used to repay social obligations.

Certain people *should* be invited: spouses or fiancés of adult relatives and friends, even if you don't know them; the spouses or fiancés of the bridal party; the cleric or officiant and spouse; and brothers and sisters of the bride and groom.

"What about people who are living together?" you may ask. Invite them both if you possibly can. Small children are generally not included in a formal or semi-formal affair, particularly if it is held in the evening. (Note how to invite or not to invite children in the following section on invitations.)

There is one other major consideration in devising the guest list, and that is the issue of space. You must be sure that the locations you have chosen for the ceremony and reception can accommodate the number of people you intend to invite. You want your guests to be comfortable, and you don't want to violate fire codes! Even if you're planning an outdoor wedding on three acres of rolling lawn, think about what will happen if it rains.

Once you've managed to pare down the list to everyone's satisfaction, what next? You must set up a system for keeping track of invitations and responses.

Start by having each family make its guest list on separate index cards so the final list can easily be alphabetized. Request complete names, addresses, and zip codes. Phone numbers are also helpful for contacting tardy repliers. Make sure these cards are given to you by a certain deadline. Then compare these names with your own, check for any duplications and inaccuracies, and compile one master list.

On that list you will want to note whether guests are to receive an invitation or an announcement. Later you'll also need room to note responses so you can keep a current count for the caterer and can check up on those who have been delinquent in replying. (Admittedly you shouldn't have to do this, but some people don't realize how important it is to respond promptly.)

You can buy special planning books for this kind of record keeping at your bookstore or stationer or through the pages of *Modern Bride*, but a plain spiral notebook or three-by-five-inch index cards will do just as well. By a week before the wedding you should have all the responses and a final count for the reception.

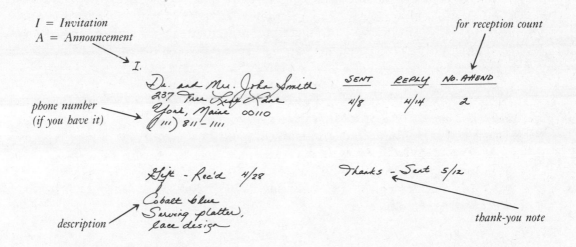

Choosing Invitations

The invitation is the first indication of the style of your wedding. Today's traditional and contemporary invitations offer a wide variety of options to set the tone you want to project.

As soon as the date is set and the guest lists are completed, select and order your invitations—at least three months before the wedding to allow ample time for mailing and delivery. Invitations can be ordered from a jeweler, stationer, department store, or specialty advertiser. All have consultants and/or samples to aid you in the choice of paper, color, style of lettering, and correct wording, especially for difficult family situations.

The most elegant, formal, and expensive invitations are engraved on white or off-white stock. Thermography is a process that yields a raised print resembling engraving. It is less expensive than engraving, more frequently used, and perfectly appropriate for formal or semiformal weddings. Printed, telephoned, or handwritten invitations are acceptable for the informal wedding. When in doubt about selection, opt for the more conservative, traditional approach.

Wedding invitations are sent from four to six weeks prior to the wedding date and should all be mailed at the same time. Envelopes should be handwritten in black ink, never typed; do not abbreviate names or addresses. These days response cards and a stamped, preaddressed envelope are usually included to assure the receipt of a reply. (If you can rely on your friends and relatives to abide by the tradition of handwriting a prompt response to a formal invitation, you don't need these.) Be advised that there are size restrictions in the postal service, so make sure your reply envelopes are not too small. Take one invitation with all the enclosures to the post office to be weighed so you will know what postage is required.

The inner envelope is left unsealed and is addressed to say, Mr. and Mrs. Johnson, without first names or addresses. If you wish to invite their children under sixteen, write the children's first names in a line below their parents' on the inner envelope. Older children in the family should receive separate invitations. The phrase "and family" is never used. Note that if you do not name the children here, or invite them separately, then they are clearly *not* invited to the wedding.

There are several enclosures you may include, particularly if you are having a large, formal wedding:

Reception Cards: Even when everyone on your list is invited to both the ceremony and the reception, a special reception card is often enclosed carrying the words "the pleasure of your company . . . " It is also proper just to simply put the information about the reception right on the wedding invitation with something like "reception immediately following at . . . "

Ceremony Cards: These are used when more people are invited to the reception than to the wedding ceremony. In that case, the invitation is to the reception, and the enclosure is for the ceremony. The format of the two is essentially reversed.

Pew Cards: Seldom is an affair so large or formal that one would be required to prove that he was invited. But should you be planning a truly elaborate wedding, pew cards would read: "Please present this card at Saint John's Church on Saturday, the fifth of May."

RSVP Cards with stamped, addressed envelopes: These cards should be ready to mail to your parents or whoever hosts the wedding. Guests simply check a line indicating whether they will or will not attend.

If your invitations contain several enclosures, the proper order of placement is as follows: tuck the response cards, and any other enclosures, in their accompanying envelopes; put all enclosures inside the invitation; place tissue paper over the engraving or printing on the invitation to ensure against smudging; tuck the invitation, fold side down, into the ungummed envelope; put the ungummed envelope in the outer envelope so it faces the flap. If you plan to include a map, be sure it is a clear reproduction on quality paper. This also belongs inside the invitation with the other enclosures.

Wording of Invitations

Traditionally, when the bride's parents host the wedding, the invitation is issued in their name. Today there are many other variations. The samples shown below will help you choose the appropriate wording for your invitations. The date, time, and place appear after the names. Note one special convention: the words "the honour of your presence" (always spelled with the British *u*) on the invitation indicate a religious ceremony, while the words "the pleasure of your company" indicate a civil service.

If you have any really unusual circumstances or special problems, discuss them with your stationer. He has the knowledge and the experience to help you with correct form and proper wording. If your circumstances are more unique than this expert can handle, use common sense and you'll do just fine.

This is how your invitation would traditionally read if your parents are hosting the wedding:

Mr. and Mrs. Lloyd Douglas
request the honour of your presence
at the marriage of their daughter
Catherine Ann
to
Charles Andrew Grey
Saturday, the fourteenth of June
St. Peter's Roman Catholic Church
Chappaqua, New York

Here are some variations in the wording appropriate to the following situations:

PARENTS SHARE PLANNING

Mr. and Mrs. Lloyd Douglas
request the honour of your presence
at the marriage of their daughter
Catherine Ann
to
Charles Andrew Grey
son of Mr. and Mrs. Michael Grey

YOU TWO ARE THE HOSTS

The honour of your presence
is requested at the marriage of
Catherine Ann Douglas
to
Charles Andrew Grey

YOUR REMARRIED PARENTS HOST

Mrs. Alan Crane
and
Mr. Lloyd Douglas
request the honour of your presence
at the marriage of their daughter
Catherine Ann
to
Charles Andrew Grey

HIS PARENTS ARE HOSTS

Mr. and Mrs. Michael Grey
request the honour of your presence
at the marriage of
Catherine Ann Douglas
to their son
Charles Andrew Grey

ONE REMARRIED PARENT HOSTS

Mr. and Mrs. Alan Crane
request the honour of your presence
at the marriage of her daughter
Catherine Ann
to
Charles Andrew Grey

YOUR DIVORCED PARENTS HOST*

Mrs. Pamela Douglas*
and
Mr. Lloyd Douglas
request the honour of your presence
at the marriage of their daughter
Catherine Ann
to
Charles Andrew Grey

* If your mother has assumed her maiden name, use "Ms. Pamela Griffen and Mr. Lloyd Douglas."

Announcements

Announcements are sent to those you would have liked to have had at your wedding and reception but couldn't. Sending announcements is a thoughtful way to share your happy news with professional associates, distant relatives, and faraway friends. They do not obligate the recipient to send a gift, though many people will acknowledge the event with a card or note.

The announcement can be issued by the bride's family, the groom's family, or the couple themselves. The wording is similar to the wording of an invitation except that "have the honour to announce" or "have the pleasure of announcing" appears in place of the invitational request. (The distinction between "honour" and "pleasure" is not so important in an announcement.)

Announcements are generally in the same tone or style as your invitations. They are ordered when invitations are ordered, and are sent out on the wedding day (never before) or as soon after that day as possible. Obviously, announcements are never sent to anyone who was invited to the wedding.

At-home cards may be included with your announcements. These carry your new address after marriage and the date on which you will be in residence. They can also be a good opportunity to let everyone know if you will continue to use your own name after the wedding.

One final tip about both invitations and announcements: when you order, ask about getting the envelopes in advance so you can have them all addressed and ready to go when the invitations come in.

Thank-You Notes

Years ago, formal thank-you notes, or "personals," were ordered along with the invitations and announcements. They had the bride's formal, married name, "Mrs. John E. Doe," on the overleaf, because it was presumed that she would be writing all the notes of appreciation for the wedding gifts. You can still order formal notes if you wish. But more than likely you and your fiancé will *both* be writing thank-you notes, so you will need stationery you can both use.

Somehow there's something very enticing about beautiful writing paper. No doubt when you visit your stationer's to order invitations, you will be overwhelmed by the selection of note cards, writing paper, embossed envelopes, and gift acknowledgment and gift enclosure cards—all sporting your new name or initials, of course. Fine personal stationery has a wonderfully rich feel, but good quality is never cheap, and you must remember your budget.

If you can't resist and have the money to spend, great! It's worth it. If not, plain white or pastel note cards—even paper by the pound—will be quite proper. Stay away from gimmicky selections, ornately embellished with wild colors and designs. Even with your thank-yous, you want to maintain the more dignified tone of your wedding.

The four most important words about thank-you notes are YOU MUST WRITE THEM! And you should do so as quickly as possible. If you've had a huge wedding of over two hundred guests, printed gift acknowledgment cards are permissible *for acknowledgment only*. They still must be followed by personal, hand-written notes from you or your husband.

Just about everyone gets a thank-you note, and it should be written within four months after the wedding. Notes go to all who gave you a gift, even the individual parties who gave a combined gift, unless it's an office group where your note can be circulated or displayed for all to see. You'll also want to remember those who did special things for you, your attendants, relatives who played host to out-of-town guests, etc.

Thank-you notes don't have to be long, but they should be as personal as possible. Mention your husband's (wife's) name, the specific gift, what you particularly like about it, and even how you will use it. Here's an example:

Dear Jody and Bob,

Dan and I are dazzled in every sense of the word by the Waterford decanter! It looks stunning with the family crystal, and will always grace the table for our most special guests. You two are at the top of the list, of course!

Thank you bunches! Let's get together soon.

Love,

Some might take more thought than others, particularly if you don't really like the gift or if you have no idea what it is. In any case, concentrate on the warm feelings you have for the giver and your appreciation for his or her thoughtfulness as you compose your note. Here's another example:

Dear Aunt Faye,

What an original idea for a wedding gift! John and I were delighted to receive such a welcome addition to our first home. It will forever remind us of the special lady who chose it just for us.

Thank you,

Love,

No discussion of thank-you notes would be complete without the mention of the record keeping involved. Again, bridal books are available for the task, though an ordinary notebook or even your index cards will do. Just be sure to allow space for the name of the giver, the gift received with some description, and a column to date when the thank you has been sent. Combining this with your record of invitations issued is a good method; the name and address are already in place, so you need add only two columns. (See the sample on page 71.)

Guests are not supposed to bring gifts to the wedding itself, but some may. It is wise to appoint someone to record these items (your mother or another close relative) and store them safely so you don't lose track of last-minute presents.

"While I had already written many of the thank-you notes before the wedding, Bobby and I found we actually enjoyed sitting down in the evenings to do the remaining ones together," recalls Jane, now a not-so-newlywed. "We laughed about some of the gifts, really made plans for using others, and generally enjoyed reliving the whole wedding experience."

We hope you will too.

The Wedding Ceremony

*T*he ceremony that binds you and your fiancé in matrimony is the most emotional and spiritual part of your wedding day, so you will want it to reflect your heartfelt convictions about marriage and to set the tone for the celebration that follows. Honest exploration of your feelings and early planning are essential if you are to have the ceremony that best expresses the union you will strive to achieve.

An overwhelming majority (75 percent) of today's couples choose to marry in a religious ceremony. Why? The answer undoubtedly lies in more than just the attraction of the church or synagogue, many of which are quite plain. For reasons often hard to explain, even those who may not be particularly religious feel a need to somehow sanctify or elevate this momentous event, and to add another dimension to what is by law a routine civil procedure.

A religious ceremony does not have to take place in a house of worship, however. The cleric will usually agree to perform a service at your home or in any other suitably dignified location. It's not the place that determines the nature of the ceremony; it's the status of the officiant.

The wedding ceremony, whether religious or civil, can be as traditional or as nontraditional as you like, depending on how you choose to enter and exit. The classic ceremony includes: a processional, in which the bride is escorted down the center aisle (or she may walk alone) preceded by her attendants; the exchange of vows before the officiant; and the recessional, in which the happy bride and groom come back down the aisle, followed by their attendants and families. No matter what the location of the ceremony, or how large or small the actual wedding party, if a formal entrance and exit are made, the ceremony is considered traditional. (The traditional configuration of the Christian processional and recessional is illustrated on page 82; the traditional Jewish entrance and exit appear on pages 80–81.)

In nontraditional ceremonies, there is no formal processional or recessional. Lighting or music may signal that the event is about to take place, and the couple will simply emerge from the side or otherwise join together at the appointed place. Usually, when the ceremony is completed, joyful guests spontaneously rush up to congratulate the couple.

Obviously, modifications and additions can be made in either type of ceremony. The more elaborate the wedding, the more involved the protocol. Your officiant will instruct you and the members of your party at the rehearsal.

JEWISH PROCESSIONAL

1) *Bride*
2) *Groom*
3) *Maid or matron of honor (bridesmaids precede her)*
4) *Best man (ushers precede him)*
5) *Flower girl (ring bearer escorts her)*
6) *Mother of the bride*
7) *Father of the bride*
8) *Mother of the groom*
9) *Father of the groom*
10) *Rabbi and/or cantor*

DURING THE JEWISH SERVICE

1) Bride
2) Groom
3) Maid or matron of honor
4) Best man
5) Mother of the bride
6) Father of the bride
7) Mother of the groom
8) Father of the groom
9) Rabbi
10) Cantor

Note: Flower girl, ring bearer, bridesmaids, and ushers do *not* stand under the chuppah

JEWISH RECESSIONAL

1) Bride
2) Groom
3) Maid of honor (bridemaids follow her)
4) Best man (ushers follow him)
5) Flower girl (ring bearer escorts her)
6) Mother of the bride
7) Father of the bride
8) Mother of the groom
9) Father of the groom
10) Rabbi and/or cantor

1) Bride
2) Groom
3) Maid or matron of honor
4) Best man
5) Bridesmaids
6) Ushers
7) Flower girl
8) Ring bearer
9) Father of the bride
10) Cleric

1) Bride
2) Groom
3) Maid or matron of honor
4) Best man
5) Bridesmaids
6) Ushers
7) Flower girl
8) Ring bearer

CHRISTIAN PROCESSIONAL

CHRISTIAN RECESSIONAL

1) Bride
2) Groom
3) Maid or matron of honor
4) Best man
5) Bridesmaids
6) Ushers
7) Flower girl
8) Ring bearer
9) Cleric

DURING THE CHRISTIAN CEREMONY

The Civil Wedding

The civil ceremony is a legal adaptation of our Protestant forefathers' *Book of Common Prayer*. At its most perfunctory in City Hall, the whole exchange takes about one minute, not including the signing of the appropriate papers.

For many who believe that the ceremony is but an incidental legalism in the process of marriage, the simple civil procedure will do just fine, thank you. Often such couples marry without fanfare and even enlist the services of people nearby as witnesses.

However, civil ceremonies do not have to be abrupt and devoid of emotion. Many civil officiants are quite eloquent and capable of delivering lovely personal commentary on the purpose and beauty of marriage. If prior arrangements are made, most judges and justices are willing to perform the ceremony at the site of your choice, where the whole affair can be considerably enriched with music, flowers, and other classic nuptial touches.

Marriages are among the more pleasant duties of state officials, and you will find most of them eager and happy to assist you with special plans. Just be sure to give the officiant ample prior notice and to have the proper legal documents on hand for the ceremony.

The Protestant Wedding

For Christians, the wedding ceremony has special religious significance. Christ performed the first miracle of his public life at the wedding in Cana (John 2:1–12), and the relationship of Christ to his church is considered analogous to the marriage of husband and wife (Ephesians 5:23). It is not surprising, then, that these and other passages from the Old and New Testaments often form the basis of the Protestant wedding ceremony.

At its simplest, the Protestant wedding can be performed in ten minutes; at its most elaborate, the nuptial service may take an hour or more. Regardless of liturgical embellishments peculiar to individual localities and denominations, the religious ceremony consists of three parts: the introductory remarks on marriage, the exchange of vows and rings, and the final blessings of the couple. The basic ceremony may be considerably personalized by music, readings, and other additions.

With few exceptions, church rules governing Protestant marriage are primarily shaped by state laws and local practices. Because of the many Protestant denominations, however, it is impossible to generalize, so you should always check particulars with your clergy. Besides church laws, some ministers have guidelines on music, flowers, photographs, and so forth that must also be honored.

Traditionally, church weddings are not held on Sundays, out of regard for regular worship services, or on Good Friday, in deference to the death of Christ. Most ministers will perform a religious ceremony in a location other than a church, will co-officiate with other clerics, or will do whatever else they can to accommodate any special needs or wishes, provided the couple's requests are appropriate and in good taste.

With the exception of the Episcopal (Anglican) Church, marriage is not a sacrament in Protestant religions, but it is recognized as a holy and desirable union. Moreover, some faiths strongly oppose divorce as a violation of a sacred contract. The public profession of love and fidelity serves as a testament to God's plan for man, and as an inspiration to the community of the faithful. Only within such a religious context can a couple hope to achieve a truly Christian marriage.

The Roman Catholic Wedding

Since Roman Catholicism is the world's largest organized Christian religion, it is not surprising that the Catholic wedding is steeped in tradition and Canon Law. What is surprising is that it is also among the most liberal religions in accommodating individual needs of the nuptial couple.

The Catholic Church is uniform both in its regulations governing marriage and in the performance of the actual ceremony. Yet rare is the priest who will not do all in his power to solve any problems and to honor any reasonable requests. When planned properly, the Catholic wedding service is an elegant, solemn liturgy. If this is what you want, do contact your priest the moment your decision to marry has been made. There are several reasons for this.

There is considerable paperwork to be processed. There is a premarital program to be completed, and an Engaged Encounter Weekend is recommended. Most dioceses require at least six months' notice of wedding plans, and some now require a year. Public notice of the wedding, called the banns, must be published in the church bulletin of the bride's parish three consecutive Sundays before the wedding.

The Catholic wedding may or may not take place within the context of a Nuptial Mass. If it does, the actual wedding comes after the Homily and before the Offertory, and the bride and groom are already positioned at the altar.

If the wedding is held without a Mass, the bride meets the groom at the altar and the priest makes introductory remarks. He asks if the couple marries freely, to which each answers, "I do." The couple join hands and declare their vows. The priest then blesses the rings and the bride and groom exchange them. The nuptial blessing is given and the groom kisses the bride. This rite may be considerably individualized with personal readings and other added formalities.

Within a Nuptial Mass, the whole ceremony takes about an hour. Without the Mass, the ceremony is completed in roughly twenty minutes. A Nuptial Mass is recommended for the marriage of two Catholics, but a Catholic and a non-Catholic may have one if they wish. The only day in the liturgical year on which marriages are not performed is Good Friday.

Church law does not demand that the wedding take place in a church, though some individual dioceses do. Nor does it place any restrictions on music, flowers, photography, or attire. But it does emphasize the sacramental nature of marriage, and thus it expects that the dignity and solemnity of the occasion be preserved. Particular priests and pastors may have their own interpretations of dignity and solemnity, however, so local custom prevails.

The only real problem with marriage in the Catholic Church arises when one of the parties has been married before and is divorced. A declaration of nullity must be granted to render the person free to marry. Each case is handled on an individual basis, and it is advisable to be completely honest with the priest from the very beginning.

Because marriage is a sacrament in this church, and because it is indissoluble, it is officially viewed with high seriousness and extreme joy. It helps if a couple can keep these attitudes in mind while attending to the myriad details of a Roman Catholic wedding.

The Eastern Orthodox Wedding

The Eastern Orthodox faith comes to America through immigrants from Eastern Europe and the Mediterranean, where for twenty centuries it has been the dominant expression of Christianity. There are over six million members of Orthodox congregations in North America today, including the Greek, Russian, Polish, Yugoslavian, Serbian, Syrian, and other Eastern churches. Their fundamental faith reflects Christianity as taught by the Apostles and the Scripture, creeds, and liturgies of the early church. Orthodoxy is still the official state religion of Greece.

The Eastern Orthodox Church adheres strictly to ancient tradition and dogma. Thus marriage, one of the church's seven sacraments, is governed by ritual and regulation. Go see the priest as soon as your decision to marry has been made so he can process all paperwork and explain all requirements and procedures.

Holy matrimony is a most joyous occasion. It has its own form and ritual, and is not celebrated within the context of the Divine Liturgy or any other service. It begins with the Betrothal (the exchange of rings) and continues with the introductory Prayers of Petition.

The climax of the ceremony is the Crowning, which symbolizes the couple's glory and victory in reaching this moment in their lives, and their new titles as king and queen of their own kingdom, the Christian home. In the Greek Church, these crowns are made in the likeness of orange blossoms and are tied together with ribbon to symbolize the couple's unity. (Other churches may use metal crowns.)

The Crowning is followed by scriptural readings and the jubilant dance of Isaiah, in which the bride, groom, and sponsor (best man or woman), led by the priest, do a spiritual dance three times around the little Altar at the Soleas (the platform at the front of the inner sanctuary). This dance is the ultimate expression of love and joy during the ceremony. Then the final blessings are given and the ceremony is concluded.

The Orthodox wedding takes about forty-five minutes from start to finish. It must be performed in an Orthodox church, and weddings are not held on certain Holy Days and some periods in Lent. Particulars regarding music, flowers, photography, attire, and so on should be discussed with the priest.

Because marriage is a sacrament in the Eastern Orthodox Church, divorce is not encouraged. But ecclesiastical divorces are granted on several grounds, which allow a person to marry again in the church. Your priest can advise you. Also, interfaith marriages are not encouraged, but may be performed under certain conditions.

The Orthodox wedding, resplendent with its many cultural and religious customs, is a truly memorable event in the spiritual and temporal lives of all who participate.

The Jewish Wedding

The rich heritage of the Jewish faith and the personal and communal significance of the nuptial ceremony make the Jewish wedding a joyous and meaningful event for all who attend. Because Judaism is as much a culture as a religion, the ethnic flavor of the music, the dancing, the food, and all the other traditional touches add to the special character and appeal of the whole celebration. It is important, therefore, to understand and to respect the symbolic origin of the elements involved.

Ancient Jewish law prescribed that a couple marry in front of two adult male witnesses in one of three ways: that the woman accept a gift (not necessarily a ring) offered to her by a man; that a woman accept a Ketubah, the civil contract of marriage, offered by a man; or that the couple physically consummate the marriage. Today, Jewish tradition has incorporated all three of these elements into the wedding ritual.

Often escorted by their parents down the aisle, the bride and groom gather under the chuppah (symbolic of the tent in which newlyweds dwelt in ancient times), take a ceremonial sip of wine (symbolic of the first wedding or engagement), and receive a blessing from the rabbi. The bride then immediately accepts her ring (a plain gold one with no stones, so as to not be misled by the groom's wealth), the first official act of the wedding ceremony. Next is the reading of the Ketubah (a precursor of today's marriage contracts delineating the groom's obligations to the bride, including property settlements). Though this document has now become a rather standardized version of the ancient individualized contract, its presentation by the groom to the bride is the second major event in the wedding.

This is followed by the Seven Blessings, traditionally given by special guests or family members, a second sip of wine (symbolic of the actual or second wedding), and the climactic breaking of the glass to the happy cries of "Mazel tov!" (Universally recognized as a symbol of Jewish marriage, the breaking of the glass is a reminder of the fragility of life and echoes the destruction of the Temple at Jerusalem.) The couple then retires to a private room (Yihud) for a few minutes, symbolizing the consummation of the marriage, before the festivities begin.

The entire ceremony, including the rabbi's address, takes about twenty minutes. The basic ritual outlined above is followed in Orthodox and many Conservative weddings. Reform Jews have changed and adapted the ceremony a bit to incorporate modern preferences and customs. There may, for instance, be a double-ring ceremony. The couple may use special poems and readings. Even the "Do you take this man/woman . . . I do" part of the ceremony is an addition of a strictly American civil custom.

From a religious standpoint, there is no minimum engagement period required by the Jewish faith. Practical considerations, however, make it advisable to plan several months in advance. Some couples may wish to fashion a very special or elaborate chuppah under which to be married. Likewise, some want their Ketubah artistically rendered for prominent display in their future homes. These things take time. And the rabbi, the synagogue, the musicians, the caterers, and others may have conflicting schedules. As always, then, the earlier you contact the rabbi, the better.

There is one other consideration for divorced women seeking to remarry in the Jewish faith, and that pertains to the get. Divorce is not illegal under Jewish law; indeed, provisions are made for it. But Orthodox and Conservative rabbis will not marry an agunah, or bound woman. Even in some Reform circles, a woman who has not been given a get, a rabbinical document of dissolution of a former marriage, may want to contemplate the ramifications of remarrying without it. In any event, leave time to discuss this matter with your rabbi.

Weddings are not held on Shabbat and certain other major Holy Days. There are some additional restrictions governing the marriages of widows and of relatives, and some special requirements of the two marriage witnesses. Again, your rabbi is your best advisor.

Except for questions of appropriateness, there are no real restrictions on location, music, flowers, or attire. The bride may wear a veil, though it must be off the face for the ceremony (lest the groom, like Jacob of old, marry the wrong woman). Some Orthodox communities have religious strictures against all picture taking, but most rabbis allow, even encourage, photographs.

A final word on Jewish wedding ritual comes from a Reform rabbi: "Stomp a glass, not a flashbulb, at the end of the ceremony. Flashbulbs are tacky!"

The Nonsectarian Wedding

Nonsectarian is exactly that: not affiliated in any way with an organized religious denomination. Though usually Christian, nonsectarian churches cater to the needs of those with basic religious beliefs who cannot or will not comply with the rules and regulations imposed by more structured faiths. Their services are generally quite simple, involving preaching, scriptural readings, personal witness, and music.

Nondenominational churches and interfaith chapels are often the best choices for those who want a religious wedding ceremony but who do not subscribe to the tenets of a particular faith. The style and structure of wedding ceremonies held in such locations vary greatly, so it is advisable to speak with individual ministers and chaplains of such congregations in your area.

Most are quite cooperative and accommodating in meeting a couple's needs, as long as a basic respect for the marriage service is preserved. Most will also perform ceremonies in locations other than their own churches.

The Military Wedding

Any enlisted man or woman or officer in any branch of the armed services, or any cadet at any of the military academies, can have a military wedding in full dress. Military weddings are a privilege of the armed services, and a distinctive, impressive event. But because of the special protocol involved, they may take additional planning.

A military wedding can be held in a base/post chapel, an academy chapel, or a civilian church. Regardless of where it takes place, certain guidelines prevail:

1. All military weddings are formal, with military personnel in full dress uniform (blue in winter, white in summer) and white gloves. Civilian members of the wedding party dress in complementary formal attire. If the bride is in the military, she may wear either her dress uniform or a traditional gown.
2. Invitations to a military wedding read the same as those to a civilian ceremony except that the groom's rank and branch are specified—for example, Captain James March, U.S. Air Force. If the bride is in the military, she does not generally show her title on the invitations, but she may if she wishes, especially if she plans to be in uniform for the wedding.
3. Seat commanding officer guests according to rank. If your ushers are in the service, they should know how to do this. If they are not in the military, consult with the officer of protocol, and instruct them accordingly.
4. The arch of swords (navy) or sabers (army) under which the bride and groom pass following the ceremony is one of the most distinctive formalities of the military wedding. This takes place as the couple leaves the church/chapel. There should be four to six saber/sword bearers, who may also be your ushers.

5.   Ceremony and reception decorations usually include the American flag and the standards of the bride's and/or groom's units, as well as traditional flowers, candles, and other items. The wedding cake is always cut by the bride and groom with the sword or saber.

Each chaplain or branch of service may have its own regulations and traditions, so it is wise to investigate particulars early in your planning. The major military academies have individual regulations as well. If you would like to have a reception at a facility connected with the academy, bookings at busy times are required *far* in advance.

You can contact the protocol officer at each academy for further information: United States Naval Academy, Annapolis, Maryland; United States Air Force Academy, Colorado Springs, Colorado; United States Military Academy, West Point, New York; United States Coast Guard Academy, Groton, Connecticut; and United States Maritime Academy, Kings Point, New York.

The Double Wedding

The double wedding doubles everything but the cost, which is a practical reason why some brides choose it. Much less in fashion now than it once was when brides were younger and more likely to be getting married at the same time in life, the double wedding can still be unique, personal, and fun.

Double weddings are most commonly chosen because the brides (or grooms) are siblings or very dear friends. The emphasis here is on the *very*! Because everything must be done in unison—same wedding style, identical male attire, similar female attire (including brides' gowns), and shared music, flowers, and fare—the two brides must be absolutely certain they can agree on all wedding details and that neither will feel upstaged or overpowered by the other. The double wedding works only if there is complete and total harmony.

Though each bride will have her own set of attendants (of equal numbers), a single invitation is issued when the brides are sisters. If they are not related, combined or separate invitations may be chosen. One bride, usually the elder, and her party proceeds down the aisle first, followed by the second wedding party and bride. Couples might also purposely choose a church or synagogue with two aisles so entrances can be made simultaneously.

At the reception, there is one receiving line if only one family is hosting, two if two separate families are involved. There may also be two bridal tables and two wedding cakes if the families prefer. Just take care there aren't too many separate touches, or the original purpose of your double wedding will be negated.

The Candlelight Wedding

The candlelight ceremony can be civil or religious, in church or at home, formal or informal. Such a service is rich in symbolism and drama, and can transform even the simplest ceremony into something quite stunning.

Candlelight ceremonies are most effective when held in the evening. Additional artificial light should be kept to a minimum, though you certainly want enough light so you can be seen! Large candle pedestals, ornate candelabra, hurricanes, or lanterns should be strategically placed where they will cast the best light and shadows but are not in danger of being extinguished by breezes or air ducts. Smartly dressed acolytes give the lighting of the candles particular interest.

At some point in the ceremony you and your parents may want to light special candles symbolizing family unity and the transference of life and love from one generation to the next. Scriptural passages, poetry, or your own prepared words can make this a loving and personal part of your wedding ceremony.

Although you might be tempted to have your attendants carry lighted candles down the aisle or your guests light candles as participants in the services, it is advisable to avoid the dangers of moving with flames. The same overall effects can be created with large numbers of candles on the altar or stationary pew markers.

However many candles you decide to use, and in whatever fashion you plan to use them, always check building fire codes and local fire ordinances first. That way you can enjoy the warm glow of your wedding in safety and good conscience.

Ceremonial Music

"I'm a pretty broad-minded fellow, but I honestly thought I would die," exclaimed an accomplished music director of a large church that does over two hundred weddings a year. "Can you imagine anyone seriously considering 'My Love Does It Good' for her wedding?"

No doubt stranger things have been heard, especially during the years when the Top Ten resounded regularly throughout wedding chapels all across America. Today, thank Mozart, the return to more traditional weddings has seen a return to more traditional music as well.

Not that wedding music has to be tired and trite. In fact, most organists and choral directors recommend compiling a program of both classical and contemporary pieces for a pleasing effect. You might even consider a small ensemble of several instruments, the trumpet, violin, flute, harp, or guitar, in addition to the piano or organ.

Many churches guarantee their organist a fee for every wedding performed there whether you use the person or not. This practice is endorsed by the American Guild of Organists and is considered professional courtesy. You will probably want to consult the music director of your church or synagogue anyway, to be advised of any musical preferences particular to that house of worship. Guidelines and restrictions can vary considerably.

The church organist can usually recommend vocalists and other musicians. Be prepared to pay each of them the standard performance fee for your area—more

Popular Wedding Music

Here is a list of some of the most popular wedding music used today. For more information and recommendations, contact: American Guild of Organists, New York, New York; National Association of Pastoral Musicians, Washington, D.C.; or North American Liturgy Resources, Phoenix, Arizona.

CLASSICAL

"Bridal Chorus" from *Lohengrin*	Richard Wagner
"Wedding March" from *A Midsummer Night's Dream*	Felix Mendelssohn
"Prince of Denmark's March" (Often incorrectly called "Trumpet Voluntary" by Purcell)	Jeremiah Clarke
"Trumpet Tune"	Henry Purcell
"The Rondo"	Jean Joseph Mouret
"St. Anthony Chorale" (arranged by Brahms)	Franz Joseph Haydn
Selections from the Water Music Suite	George Friedrich Handel
Psalm XIX	Benedetto Marcello
"Now Thank We All Our God" for trumpet and organ (arranged by E. Power Biggs)	J. S. Bach
"Bridal March"	C. H. Perry
"Ave Maria" (or the more flourishing Bach-Gounod arrangement)	Franz Schubert
Canon in D Major (arranged for organ)	Johann Pachelbel
"Ode to Joy" from Ninth Symphony	Ludwig van Beethoven
"Radetsky March" (arranged by J. Farrell)	Johann Strauss
March from *Judas Maccabaeus*	George Friedrich Handel

CONTEMPORARY

"Perhaps Love"	John Denver
"We've Only Just Begun"	Paul Williams
"Evergreen"	Barbra Streisand *and* Paul Williams
"What I Did for Love"	Marvin Hamlisch
"You Needed Me"	Randy Goodrum
"Feelings"	Morris Albert
"The Wedding Song"	Paul Stokey

All the favorites from Broadway musicals: "If I Loved You," "You'll Never Walk Alone," "Climb Every Mountain," "The Wedding March," "Sunrise, Sunset," "The Sabbath Prayer," "If We Only Have Love," "One Hand, One Heart," and many others.

if a good deal of rehearsal will be involved for your selections. If no organist is available, check with the music departments of local colleges, the local musicians' union, music stores, or symphony groups, or look through the Yellow Pages. Be sure that you are familiar with any selections to be played, and that you have personally heard the musicians and vocalists who will be performing on your wedding day.

People are often intimidated by their own lack of musical knowledge and thus are tempted to leave it all up to the musicians. If you do that, you forfeit your right to shape one of the most influential elements of your wedding. Music sets a tone, creates an atmosphere. On your wedding day, it reflects you.

You will need to plan for twenty to thirty minutes of pre-ceremony music while guests are being seated, to decide on a processional and a recessional, and to have one or more selections during the service. You don't *have* to go down the aisle to Wagner's "Bridal Chorus" or Mendelssohn's "Wedding March," but you do need entrance and recessional selections with appropriate rhythm.

Many of the most popular classical selections are available on a record from R.C.A. called "The Wedding Album." If you can't find the album at your local record store or public library, write to RCA Records, 1133 Avenue of the Americas, New York, NY 10036.

Interfaith Marriage

The basic problem in interfaith marriage stems from the premise that if two people don't share the same religious values and beliefs, they cannot enter into a valid religious contract of marriage. Some faiths have resolved such ideological difficulties, others haven't. Briefly, this is what to expect from the major world religions on the question of interfaith marriage.

Buddhist: Marriage is a civil matter not outlined in Buddhist scripture. A monk traditionally blesses the couple before or after the ceremony, but interfaith marriage is not a religious issue.

Hinduism: Interfaith marriage is not advocated, but does take place under certain circumstances. Check with the pujari (Hindu priest).

Judaism: Strict Judaic law does not recognize the validity of a contract between a Jew and a non-Jew. Some Reform rabbis, however, will perform an interfaith ceremony.

Mormon: Mormons may marry outside the faith, but if they do, they may not marry in a Mormon temple. Since marriage is forever, into eternity, divorce is unthinkable.

Moslem: The Koran, the book of Islamic law, classifies Moslems, Christians, and Jews as believers in the true God and therefore acceptable for intermarriage. By extension, a Moslem may also marry a practicing Buddhist or Hindu.

Eastern Orthodox: Interfaith marriage is not encouraged, but dispensation may be granted provided the non-Orthodox party is a Christian baptized in the name of the Holy Trinity.

Protestant: Some conservative Protestant groups will not perform a marriage between a Protestant and a non-Christian, and the Episcopal Church has rules about divorce and remarriage. Check with the minister of your denomination.

Roman Catholic: Routine dispensations are granted for a Catholic party to marry someone of another faith, Christian or not, provided that person is considered free to marry by the Roman Catholic Church. Each case is handled on an individual basis, so check with the priest.

There are often more than just the obvious religious differences involved in interfaith marriage. Related questions of values and customs must be answered between the two of you with the help of the cleric.

Personalized Vows

Many couples want to personalize their wedding ceremonies by writing their own vows, having additional speakers, or including family members in the ceremony. Provided the basic exchange as required by the state remains intact, most clerics and civil officiants are agreeable to a couple's wishes and may even be able to offer guidelines and suggestions based on past experience.

The first step, of course, is to check with them. Have some idea of the kinds of things you'd like to do or say, and find out just how much latitude you have for individualization.

Next you will both want to begin to solidify your thoughts. Look for books of an informational or inspirational nature in your local library, make notes of meaningful song lyrics and quotes you hear or remember, jot down your feelings about love, marriage, and commitment. You may even consider adapting passages from the Bible or other poetic works. Sometimes a different translation of the Bible will shed new light on a passage and make it more significant to you. Once you have some of your own feelings down on paper, you and your fiancé will be better able to discuss them and to decide what is appropriate and important.

From there, the two of you will ultimately have to write a script. Secure the officiant's approval, and get the sequence and timing established. Anyone else who is participating should be given a copy of the ceremony, and all final details should be worked out at the wedding rehearsal.

Make sure you take the time to practice and that your delivery is natural and sincere. Speak rather than read your vows, and don't ask anyone to do or say anything that makes him or her uncomfortable. Even though everything has been planned and rehearsed, it should all appear effortless and spontaneous.

Your Wedding Day

No matter what kind of ceremony you're having, the cardinal rule for your wedding day is GIVE YOURSELF PLENTY OF TIME! If you are having your hair done, arrange to do so early in the day. You'll want to begin dressing about two hours before the ceremony.

If the place where you are having the cermony has provided dressing rooms, everyone can get coordinated there. Otherwise you will want to have your brides-maids meet you for pictures about an hour before the nuptials. Ushers should also arrive an hour early, don their boutonnieres, and be ready to seat guests. For

Christian ceremonies, friends and relatives of the bride are seated on the left side of the church and those of the groom on the right. This practice is reversed for Jewish ceremonies.

Prelude music begins twenty to thirty minutes before the ceremony. The groom and the best man will also arrive about this time. They will meet with the officiant, who checks the marriage license, receives his fee, and makes sure the best man has the ring.

If not already present, bridesmaids and immediate family arrive about ten minutes before the ceremony. With five minutes left, the groom's parents are seated. The mother of the bride is always seated last. The officiant, the groom, and the best man take their places, the processional music resounds, and the wedding party enters. The ceremony begins!

If your wedding is smaller and less traditional, you will adjust protocol to fit your circumstances. But you'll still want to allow yourself plenty of time to get ready and to be sure that key members of your wedding party know when and where they are expected. (See "Attendants' Duties" on page 96 for more detailed information on wedding-day activities.)

Attendants' Duties

MAID/MATRON OF HONOR

Before the Wedding:

Do some of the phone or footwork, checking out competitive prices and packages for services you are considering. Help address invitations and stuff envelopes. Plan a shower or party for the couple. The bride's attendants may want to give a collective gift that can be engraved with their names or initials in addition to optional separate presents. The honor attendant makes that selection with the group's approval.

The Wedding Day:

Arrive early to help bride finish packing. Assist her in buttoning up and any other dressing details. If the bride is giving the groom a ring, keep it until the exchange at the ceremony. Hold the bride's bouquet during the service, adjust her veil and train, sign the marriage license. Stand next to the groom in the receiving line, mingle at the reception, and offer a toast to the couple. Finally, help the bride change into her going-away outfit and be sure the best man places all her luggage in the car.

BRIDESMAIDS

Before the Wedding:

Phone bride regularly, offering to do errands. Help address and stuff envelopes for invitations and announcements. Give a shower for the bride or a party for the couple.

The Wedding Day:

Be on time and keep calm. Be charming in the receiving line and circulate during the reception.

THE BEST MAN

Before the Wedding:

Take charge of making arrangements for the bachelor dinner when the male attendants and close friends of the groom are hosting. Select the collective gift presented to the groom at the dinner. Confirm the honeymoon travel reservations the day before the wedding and make sure the groom has the tickets. Provide transportation to get the groom to the ceremony.

The Wedding Day:

Arrive early to help the groom dress and finish packing. Be sure the car is parked in a strategic spot for a smooth getaway and put the luggage in it. See that the bride's luggage is placed there too. Sign the marriage license as a witness. Get the fee for the cleric from the groom and render payment at the appropriate time. Keep the bride's ring until the groom requires it at the ceremony. Offer first toast at reception. Read telegrams. Dance with the bride, honor attendant, bridesmaids, and mothers. Bring car up to take the newlyweds away.

USHERS

Before the Wedding:

Call and offer the groom whatever assistance he might need. Be cooperative about getting fitted for the formalwear. Pay attention at the rehearsal. Study the reserved seating list.

The Wedding Day:

Be at the ceremony one hour before the service begins to become familiar with any special seating arrangements and to receive boutonnieres. Be polite and take the job seriously by offering your right arm to the women as they arrive. Those with reserved seats will either show their card or tell you. If others do not inform you whether they are guests of the bride or groom, ask and escort them to a seat on the left side for the bride or on the right side for the groom. Immediately before the ceremony, two ushers will be assigned to seat the mother of the groom, then the mother of the bride. After the ceremony, the ushers escort the mothers and close relatives from the building before other guests leave. At the reception, dance with every bridesmaid.

Reception Planning

The wedding reception is the festive celebration intended to give family and friends an opportunity to share in your joy. As with any other special social occasion, you'll want to offer food, drink, and music that make everyone relaxed and happy. As we mentioned in Part I, deciding on the type and style of a wedding is bound to be much easier when all share similar backgrounds and expectations. But when that isn't the case, as it so often isn't these days, the reception logistics can present a considerable challenge.

Most of your family and friends drink beer, but you'd die before you had a keg at the country club? His large family expects robust food and ethnic dancing, while your more sedate relatives prefer champagne and chamber music? How do you solve such dilemmas? By employing *Modern Bride*'s three Cs: consideration, communication, and compromise.

If you can get everyone involved to agree generally on the size and type of reception, and if you can find yourself a competent, caring caterer or banquet manager, then half your battle is over. To accomplish those two objectives, however, you will have to talk to a great many people, do a lot of personal investigating, and really familiarize yourself with what is available within your budget. Here is a rundown of reception sites you might consider and an overview of what they offer.

The Catering Establishment

Often called catering halls or houses, these establishments are mainly in the party business, though some may also operate an adjoining restaurant. Whatever the occasion, whatever the size of your party, whatever time of day and type of affair you're giving, the catering establishment can do it all. You can even hold your wedding ceremony on the premises.

Because of the size of such establishments, they are able to accommodate larger parties, up to three hundred or more, in a variety of settings. They may have garden rooms with open terraces, formal rooms with crystal chandeliers, or clubby rooms with fireplaces. They can offer buffet or sit-down service for brunch, lunch, or dinner, with a full complement of correlated services.

Typically, the caterer will give you a package price based on a cost per person, or per head. Depending on what you choose, this can include the food and beverages, the waiters, bartenders, extra attendants, the music and flowers, the room rentals and all equipment fees, even the photographer and a master of ceremonies. If you do not have an officiant, they can often arrange for that too. Sometimes such packages make sense, as they offer the services of experienced professionals at prices much lower than if you were to contract each individually.

Establishments that do not offer all these services in-house can often recommend professionals with whom they've worked. Conversely, if you already have your own florist or musicians in mind, be sure you won't be charged for any in-house services you don't use.

Above all you must deal with a reputable establishment, one you've had experience with yourself through another affair or one that has been recommended to you. Mr. Sandy Zweben, owner of the well-known Shadowbrook in southern New Jersey, gives this advice: "Plan to visit with your fiancé and a family member, maybe more than once. Be sure you see all the rooms and settings and have a clear understanding of what is offered. Sometimes you can even arrange to hear music or sample foods. When everything is agreed, you'll be asked to sign a contract and put down a deposit (usually 10 percent), with the remainder payable in increments before the wedding. Make sure *everything* is spelled out in detail: that the types and quantities of foods and beverages are specified; that professional services and times are delineated (musicians will play for ___ number of hours, dinner will be served at ___ o'clock, the photographer will photograph every table, etc.); that the escalator clause (to allow for price increases between now and the wedding date) has a ceiling (5 to 10 percent) so that you know what it will ultimately cost; and that you understand the refund policy should you have to call off the wedding. If a caterer refuses you such information or if there is any uneasiness on your part, take your business elsewhere."

For all the amenities they offer, the catering establishment still may not be for you. First of all, it isn't cheap. While there are packages available in various price ranges, you must realize that you are paying for convenience, service, and expertise. Second, most of these establishments are very large, and your wedding may be just one of several affairs going on simultaneously. The atmosphere and service may seem less personal than in a smaller setting. Third, popular places are booked far in advance, sometimes up to two years in advance for a Friday or Saturday night, and you will pay a premium price for peak days and seasons. Lastly, because they deal in volume, some may not handle small groups at all.

Investigate. It's the only way you'll know if this type of reception is for you and your guests.

The Hotel

Each hotel has its own ambiance and personality. When you choose to hold your wedding reception in a hotel, the affair will undoubtedly assume some of the character of that particular establishment. If it is modest in size and facilities, it will have limited offerings at moderate prices; if it is grand in atmosphere and reputation, it will provide an impressive selection of services within a broad price range.

One of the best things about considering a hotel is that you can experience it before you commit yourself. You can dine and dance there, wander around and get the feel of the place, observe the staff and the clientele, or even stay overnight as a guest. Now this kind of research can be fun!

You will want to deal with the banquet manager, sometimes called the catering director or the director of special events, when making your hotel reception arrangements. Like any other caterer, this expert is experienced in handling the fare and flow of large social events (though even big hotels may also host small groups). The banquet manager will show you what is available, will discuss your wedding size, style, and budget, and will then draw up a detailed proposal for your particular affair. (Rarely are there set packages, except at large, convention-type hotels.) As a rule, hôteliers are confident of the quality and individuality of their services and will cheerfully encourage you to do some comparison shopping with their proposal in hand.

Unquestionably it is the hotel atmosphere and the personalized touch of an experienced innkeeper that makes working with a hotel so satisfying. Lorenzo Pizzia, director of catering at the internationally famous Mark Hopkins in San Francisco, says it beautifully: "A fine hotel has a tradition of excellence to uphold. We are part of the community; our clients are also our guests and our neighbors. A wedding at the Mark Hopkins is a very special event for us all. Because we can be flexible and can offer many choices, each wedding is personally arranged according to the needs and wishes of the particular couple."

Like Mr. Zweben of the Shadowbrook, Mr. Pizzia also cautions a couple to be sure they have a tangible proposal, that they understand exactly what they are getting, and that they've asked about the refund policy. Rather than incorporating an escalator clause in the contract, hotels usually figure a 5 to 10 percent price increase into their cost estimate (reputable ones like the Mark Hopkins will refund for expenses not realized later). Hotels should also be booked early, eight to twelve months in advance, and will require a 10 percent deposit when the agreements are signed. Don't forget to inquire about extras: discounted lodgings for out-of-town guests, special wedding-night rates for the bride and groom, and so forth.

If you think a hotel reception is for everyone, think again. There are some reasons why it might not be for you. First, it can be expensive, especially at a really elegant establishment. Also hotels will not usually provide musicians, florists, and photographers, though they may have recommendations. Guest parking can be problematic and costly (and you should pick up the tab). And if the hotel does a large convention/banquet business, you could find your wedding reception competing with the mirth of two thousand Brothers of the Blue Fox next door.

As we said before, it's all up to you. If you just love that grand old nineteenth-century inn, if just being there makes you feel special, then maybe that's the perfect place for your special day.

The Private Club

People choose private clubs for wedding receptions because the club plays a very significant role in their social lives, or because the club has the best—or the only—facilities for a wedding in the community. Like a hotel, a private club has a certain personality, one that mirrors the character and activities of its membership.

Although the large, full-service resort or country clubs will be exceptions to this rule, most private clubs cater to the particular needs of a select clientele: athletic, social, professional, alumni, or family. Their facilities are designed with those needs in mind, so you cannot always expect the same full line of services and accommodations that you might find at a different kind of location. Some provide space only; you'll have to provide the caterer, musicians, and so on. Others can do food and beverage service, but only within their own space and style limitations. Still others can do much more. Whatever the case, be sure you know exactly what is available and what price quotations include.

You will probably be dealing directly with the club manager or perhaps with a banquet manager. Usually you or someone in your family will have to be a member in order to arrange a club affair, though some are happy to allow nonmembers to use their facilities for special occasions. Only you can be the judge of whether you and your guests will be comfortable at a club to which you do not belong. At any rate, nothing is risked by inquiring.

The Inverness in Toledo, Ohio, is one of the nation's oldest and most respected country clubs. It is best-known for having hosted several U.S. Open Golf Championships, and the PGA Tournament is currently scheduled there for 1986. Yet this is a full-service country club with a membership of over four hundred and fifty families, many of whom have belonged for generations.

In a city like Toledo, with many other options available, why does one choose the Inverness for a wedding? "The club is elegant, well staffed, and personal," says banquet manager Eleanor Brzozka, who knows all but the newest members by name. "We know what people like and what they need, and we can work closely with them to achieve a very individual style. There's no intimidation in dealing with us because we're not strangers; we share an ongoing role in each other's lives."

Because private clubs are dealing with members, in most cases there are no formal contracts as such. But clubs will draw up proposals and give price estimates. In planning very far in advance, it is probably a good idea to have some sort of agreement in writing just to ensure against future misunderstandings.

The Restaurant

"I had my own wedding reception here," says Roy F. Guste, Jr., proprietor of the world-famous Antoine's, a New Orleans culinary landmark since 1840. "It was an intimate gathering of eight hundred of our nearest and dearest," he laughs, "not exactly the sort of thing Antoine's is known for."

What Antoine's *is* known for is French Creole cuisine impeccably prepared and artistically served. The wedding receptions hosted in this impressive French Quarter establishment are sit-down dinners for guests who appreicate fine dining.

Mr. Guste, a consummate restaurateur and author of two cookbooks, explains why: "A restaurant's emphasis is on quality food and service, and regular customers are the backbone of the business. Antoine's has been serving some families for generations. When these people choose to celebrate a special event here, it is because Antoine's is their personal preference."

When investigating restaurants, you will find that owners and managers belong to a select group of talented, creative professionals who enjoy discussing what they know best—food. They love people, especially those who value the culinary arts, and are determined that each meal in their establishment be a gastronomic delight.

A fine restaurant is an ideal reception choice for the smaller, semiformal or informal wedding. Though some can serve up to a hundred guests comfortably, most have private party rooms for groups of under fifty. It may even be possible to enlist the main dining room during off hours. Restaurants vary considerably in their handling of private parties so you'll have to get specific guidelines from those that interest you.

Restaurateurs are always happy to discuss their menus and prices. If your reception is very small, you may want to let each guest order what he prefers. If your guest list is over twenty-five, it may be easier to preorder or to limit guest choices to two or three entrée items. Cost is figured the same way as any dinner party would be—that is to say, food, bar, taxes, and gratuities—though there may be some special extra amenities offered for private parties. Although you may find the occasional exception, most restaurants serve in the seated banquet style rather than in the buffet style.

Besides the obvious size restraints, a restaurant may not do for you if your party cannot be assured of some privacy or if your preferences lean toward partying rather than dining. Most do not have the facilities and staff for lengthy cocktail hours followed by dinner, lively music, and dancing until the wee hours. But if you care about good food and want an intimate reception, a congenial restaurant might be just the ticket.

The Independent Caterer

Coming as he does with a complete service staff, all necessary accessories and equipment, and an exciting array of culinary wonders, the independent caterer allows you to literally take your show on the road. A sensible choice for at-home weddings, the private caterer is also required in those locations that do not provide food and beverage service on the premises.

An independent generally quotes a base price, which includes his services within a list of basic offerings for a given size group. From there you add so much per person, depending on the additional foods and services you select. Most require deposits at the time of agreement, but not all use formal contracts. Although some caterers specialize in weddings, they also handle other types of affairs, so are accustomed to a variety of entertaining styles and needs. The advantage here is that your wedding is truly personalized.

The disadvantage, however, is that you may have to work with your caterer closely and carefully over a period of time to achieve exactly what you have in mind. Since his business is food, your decisions are apt to be much more detailed than with other reception arrangements: for example, selecting hors d'oeuvres by the piece or individual platter rather than simply a general assortment for x number of guests.

Some caterers can provide liquor, music, flowers, favors, and additional niceties, while others do food and food service only. Some deal in gourmet delicacies, others in picnics and barbecues. Some are large, sophisticated operations, others are one-man shows. As always, personal recommendations and individual interviews are your best guide in choosing the caterer for you.

Art Wedding Service of Houston has enjoyed a reputation for quality and reliability in private catering since its inception in 1959. While they have orchestrated every conceivable type of affair for parties of "from two to two thousand," they have always considered weddings to be their special events. In spite of Art's tremendous growth and success over the years, owner-manager Pearl Smith still personally oversees and attends every single wedding they do.

"We are blessed with a large professional staff and have many resources at our disposal. Even so, our motto is elegance without extravagance, and we work very hard to tailor each wedding to a very personal style and budget. Even though we may be doing several weddings in one day, I am totally involved with each of my brides, and hope that each never realizes that there is any but her wedding on my mind."

In truth, Pearl Smith today is as much a wedding consultant as she is a caterer, but her pride in her work and her dedication to individualized service is typical of the independent caterer's philosophy. Her professional advice to anyone considering working with a private caterer is to be sure that all the financial agreements are clearly understood and to avoid the temptation of confusing quality with price.

The Home/Garden Wedding

A home or garden wedding is limited only by the size and style of your home or garden. Many a lovely, intimate ceremony has been held in a city apartment, and many a magnificent nuptial celebration has been enjoyed on a rolling lawn.

To be sure, the home wedding is a great deal more trouble for most families. There is the inevitable sprucing up of the homestead for the big event, the cleaning, painting, fixing, planting, and so forth. Then there is all the special equipment that must be procured: chairs, tables, lights, tents, and other accoutrements. Finally, even if most things are being deftly handled by caterers, technicians, and other professionals, you will still have to cope with people underfoot while you are trying to attend to other wedding preparations.

All of this notwithstanding, almost 10 percent of all brides and grooms choose to hold their weddings either at their own homes or at the homes of relatives or friends. You too may feel that a wedding held in your childhood home or in some other very special residential location is the ultimate in personalized choice, the exact tone and atmosphere you want to project on your wedding day. If so, here are some things to think about.

First, the at-home wedding is not necessarily any less expensive than the same type of affair held elsewhere; it can in fact be more so. You will still need to plan for seating, music, flowers, food, photography, and everything else in keeping with your wedding style, plus you will likely have to coordinate all these things yourself. Budget weddings can be accomplished at home only insofar as the bride and her family are willing to undertake the wedding preparations themselves.

Second, professional services will be particularly crucial to the success of the event. Florists and caterers, even photographers and musicians, should be called in well in advance. They will help you determine the best arrangements for an altar site, a receiving line, traffic flow, dancing, and food service, and advise you of any problem areas.

No matter how formal it is, a garden wedding usually has a more casual, homey atmosphere than weddings at other sites. Guests are surrounded by flowers and greenery, and natural flowers, greens, and fruits may also decorate the service tables and the wedding cake. The menu too, even at a sit-down affair, is often lighter, with foods carefully selected to be compatible with the limitations of an outdoor setting.

The bride and her wedding party may wish to further enhance the pastoral scene in their choice of attire. Garden hats or floral wreaths, wispy fabrics in ballerina-length gowns, and white or pastel-colored formal jackets instead of tuxedos will all add a distinctive freshness to the romantic setting.

Outdoor weddings can be truly beautiful when the weather cooperates, but you had better be ready with Plan B if it doesn't. Tents, canopies, dance floors, seating arrangements, food service, electrical equipment, lighting, and other outdoor details demand extra consideration, and none of these plans are impervious to wind, rain, or unseasonable temperatures.

Whether inside or out, you have to consider your guests. Can their cars be parked easily in your neighborhood? Will traffic flow smoothly and allow everyone to be comfortable and to enjoy the ceremony and the reception? If the answer to these questions is yes, then the home or garden wedding could be exactly right for you.

Finally, you can do it all yourself—perhaps with a little help from your relatives and friends. If you are an experienced hostess, a good organizer, and a realist about your abilities, it is certainly possible to rent partyware and equipment, prepare the food in advance, and do your own reception with some hired assistants for serving and cleaning up. You might even consider partial catering—purchasing the hors d'oeuvres or main course, then doing everything else yourself.

"My wedding was lovely in many ways," said one bride from southern Florida, "but I think the most important thing was that it was another happy memory in my own home, a place already associated with happy memories."

Other Possibilities

While the aforementioned are among the most common wedding-reception choices, they are certainly not all-inclusive. There are numerous other possibilities that might ideally suit your style and budget.

Many churches and synagogues also have facilities for receptions. Besides being conveniently located, such facilities are generally moderately priced, may include support staff, and might offer recommended florists, musicians, caterers, etc., all of whom are familiar with the specific needs and requirements of that particular location. The same holds true for community and cultural centers, women's clubs, and public meetinghouses.

Reception Fare

TIME OF DAY	TYPE OF RECEPTION
Morning	Champagne breakfast/brunch— sit-down or buffet
Midday	Champagne brunch/luncheon— sit-down or buffet
Midafternoon	Champagne buffet, hors d'oeuvres, cake and coffee
Early evening	Cocktail buffet
Evening	Cocktail dinner-dance— sit-down or buffet

Historic sites can be wonderfully different and dramatic locations, particularly for the traditional wedding. Some established historic places, such as the Old Sturbridge Village in Sturbridge, Massachusetts, can offer weddings in a chapel or meetinghouse, and a catered reception in a nineteenth-century tavern. Historic mansions, missions, parks, even restored riverboats are worth investigating with an eye for the unusual.

Outdoor weddings take advantage of the beauty of nature while offering a myriad of style possibilities. Formal gardens, museum grounds, arboretums, public parks—each can provide a lovely backdrop for formal or informal gatherings. (Just be sure you have an alternative plan for inclement weather.)

Planning Tips

Whatever you decide, here are some tips from the experts on reception planning and a handy chart (see above) to help you determine what is appropriate at different times of the day.

- After the decisions are made, put someone else in charge to act as liaison with the caterer and to handle reception details along the way. Make sure this person has a copy of the contract and is totally aware of what has been agreed upon. A mother, honor attendant, or bridesmaid could handle this chore.
- When sampling an establishment's fare in advance, make sure you taste dishes the same as or at least similar to those you would be having at your own reception.
- Find out your liability for additional charges, just in case things run beyond agreed-upon schedules or limits. Musicians, for instance, often charge higher rates for additional playing time over contract. (Continuous music costs more, but may be worth the expense.)
- Consider butler service for hors d'oeuvres rather than buffet service. This allows you to control the amount of food served and ensures against wastage.
- An open bar should include premium brands and *all* kinds of drinks, even mixed concoctions not often requested. Make sure this is the definition of what you're getting and paying for.
- Buffet service is not necessarily cheaper because it requires more variety and must be served longer. Investigate. The difference in price between buffet and sit-down service is often surprisingly slight.
- The same reception held at a different time of day or on a different day of the week can be less expensive. Explore alternatives.
- Bear in mind that prices and services vary greatly from city to city and region to region. Don't *assume* anything. Ask!

Reception Traditions

A wedding without some kind of reception, however small, would seem incomplete. There would be no one with whom to share your euphoria, no one from whom to receive congratulations. The wedding reception is society's tribute to a very special couple on their very special day.

Many couples like to start the receiving of guests at the door as guests leave the church or synagogue right after the ceremony. This is particularly thoughtful when you know that not all those present will be attending subsequent festivities. Even so, a formal receiving line takes place at the entrance to the reception.

Receiving Guests

The mother of the bride is first in the receiving line. She in turn introduces the guest to the mother of the groom, who is next. Next to her is the father of the groom, then the father of the bride, the bride, the groom, the maid/matron of honor, and finally the bridesmaids, who do not have to be in the receiving line, but usually are. Note that the best man and the groomsmen do not appear in the receiving line at formal weddings. They should be circulating among guests.

In smaller, less formal weddings, however, the men are often included in line. Also, if your family involves several sets of parents, use common sense in arranging the receiving line. You don't want to slight anyone, but you don't want to make people uncomfortable either. Besides, too extensive a receiving line ca... come tedious.

If you plan to have guests register in a bridal book, it can be on a table located near the beginning or the end of the receiving line. Somehow, signing first seems to eliminate bottlenecks, but you be the judge based on your particular floor plan.

Seating Arrangements

If your reception is strictly a stand-up affair, then you need not worry about any but occasional tables and chairs for the general convenience of your guests. But even the smallest sit-down reception requires place cards so guests can easily locate their places. At large dinners, table numbers are assigned, then guests select their own seats. Even so, you may need a host or hostess (often provided by the caterer) to assist everyone in finding their places.

Usually there is a main table, or bride's table, at which you and the groom are in full view. The bride sits to the groom's right and the best man on the other side of her. The ushers and bridesmaids are alternated in man-woman fashion around the table. The parents and clergy may be at this table, but at large receptions, the parents have their own table(s) nearby with clergy, close relatives, and friends.

Planning seating arrangements for guests at a large reception demands good social sense. Guests will be spending several hours together, and you want to be sure they enjoy one another's company. Have your mother and future mother-in-law help you determine where guests will be happiest.

Divorced and/or remarried parents can create some special seating considerations. It may be more practical to abandon traditional arrangements in the interest of harmony and compatibility. Perhaps they would prefer to be seated with friends among the guests rather than with each other. As always, your best judgment supersedes social convention.

Toasting

When everyone is seated, the champagne or sparkling wine is poured. Traditionally, the best man proposes the first toast to the bride and groom. It is customary for him to preface the toast with a few appropriate words. (They may be humorous, but should be in good taste.) Everyone except the bride and groom stands and drinks to the couple.

The groom makes the next toast to his bride. Thereafter the bride may make a toast, the parents, the maid/matron of honor, and so forth. After that, toasts may become spontaneous, scattered throughout the celebration.

If a marriage cup is being used, the bride and groom drink from it before the other toasting begins. (Not often used today, the marriage cup is a ceremonial vessel that comes in either the sterling Nuremberg style or the bowl-like French style. The bride and groom drink from it after repeating a few lines from their vows.)

Dancing

If dancing is on the agenda, then there are also traditions involved when the music begins. The first dance is reserved for the bride and groom and is usually their song. If dancing alone makes you uneasy, the two of you do not have to dance the entire number. The bride's father cuts in; the groom then leads his own mother to the floor. Shortly thereafter, the groom's father may join in with the bride's mother.

In the second dance, the bridegroom dances with his mother-in-law, the bride with her father-in-law, the bride's father with the bridegroom's mother, and the rest of the bridal party joins in. Guests may then follow.

Music during formal dancing and dining should be soft and romantic. Once the main meal is completed and the cake is cut, the musicians can pick up the tempo.

Cutting the Cake

Cutting the cake is one of a wedding's most precious moments, derived in large part from the tradition of friendship being cemented in the breaking of bread together. At any rate, the photograph of this ceremony will be one of the most cherished in your album.

If you're serving buffet style, you will probably want to cut the cake after the toasting takes place. At a sit-down reception, the time to cut the cake is after the meal. The bride and groom together make the first cut, his hand over hers, with a decorated silver knife. The piece of cake is held together; she takes the first bite, and offers him the second. This act of sharing symbolizes their lifetime of sharing ahead. Waiters will then cut and serve the rest of the cake.

Tossing the Bouquet

Occasionally the tossing of the bridal bouquet and the garter takes place next, to facilitate the exit of the bride and groom later on. But more often these rituals can be performed as the final acts of the celebration. All unmarried women are gathered together for the tossing of the bridal bouquet.

Traditionally the bride, her back to the women, tosses the bouquet over her shoulder. Today she may face them. Supposedly the one who catches it will be the next married. Next the groom removes the blue garter from the bride's leg and tosses it to an assemblage of unmarried men in the same manner.

Taking Leave

Even if you're only going upstairs to spend your wedding night in the same hotel, your formal exit is expected to signal an end to the festivities. As a practical matter, you should plan to take leave about a half hour before you know the band will cease to play or the reception site is due to be cleared.

If you are in fact going away, you and your husband will want to sneak off and change clothes. Just before that, the bouquet will be thrown and the garter tossed. After you return in travel attire, everyone will shower you with rice as you leave.

For most brides and grooms, the changing time becomes a very emotional and sentimental moment. Usually your best friends, your mother, and others close to you will come in "to help." What they really want to do is hug you, shed a tear or two, and say good-bye to your old life. Let them. Just plan for it so you don't get behind schedule in doing so.

Wedding Attire

Modern life offers fewer and fewer opportunities to really dress up. When most of us think back on the formal occasions in our lives, those which required long gowns and tuxedos, we recall proms, weddings, and maybe an extra-special New Year's Eve or two.

The resurgence in popularity of the formal wedding may reflect not only a return to more traditional values but also a nostalgia for some of the grace and elegance of a bygone era. And while clothes don't make the man, who could deny that when we *feel* beautiful, we *are* beautiful.

Since a wedding is one of life's landmark occasions, it is not surprising that so much concern is placed on attire that will do justice to the event. And since the bride's choice is the pivotal one around which all other selections are made, we will start with her decisions.

Bridal Gowns

Once you've determined what kind of wedding you will have—classic formal, formal, semiformal, or informal—you can start to research the bridal styles that will fit your theme.

To begin, look through the pages of *Modern Bride*. Next make a list of bridal boutiques or department stores in your area that enjoy a good reputation or that have been recommended personally by friends. Make appointments with the bridal consultants or salespeople in these shops and be prepared to discuss your wedding plans: the date you need the dress (for portraits), the type of wedding you are having, the style of dress that appeals to you, and the price range you have in mind.

The average bride spends between $400 and $600 on her wedding dress, but it is possible to find gowns for from $200 to $5,000 or more. Keep in mind that the gown is not your sole expense; the headpiece and veil and proper undergarments and accessories will all be needed to complete the outfit. Regardless of whether your budget is limited or liberal, you'll want to start early to be assured of finding just the right gown for your special day.

For the most part, wedding dresses are custom-ordered. Most stores recommend that you place your order at least six months in advance. If you're pressed for time, a dress can sometimes be obtained more quickly, depending on the manufacturer's production schedule.

The store will order your dress to the nearest size and then have it custom-fitted when it comes in. Some shops may include the cost of one fitting in the gown, but be prepared to pay for all alterations. Your order requires an initial deposit, often in cash or by bank card, no personal checks. (The same applies when the dress is picked up.) Occasionally you may be able to cancel your order within a few days, but, usually, once the gown is ordered, it must be purchased. Discuss any questions you have up front and read the purchase agreement carefully before signing it.

Fashion Facts

A sense of style and fashion flair are as important when choosing a bridal gown as when picking any other outfit. You want to pick a look appropriate to the tone of your wedding but also flattering to your facial features and body type.

Each fall and spring, bridal designers introduce their new lines. Like other fashion collections, these lines integrate new design concepts into the predictable needs of the marketplace. While certain trends and looks may come and go, some basic bridal facts can help you make a selection from all that's available.

First, recognize your body type. Some gowns can overpower a woman, make her fade away in a bundle of ruffles and lace. Others are simply not enough, do not enhance her size or stateliness. On your wedding day, of all days, you want to put your best fashion foot forward. The following guidelines will prove helpful:

Short and Thin: A high-rise waistline, floor-length veil, high neckline, chapel-length train—perhaps sleeveless with long gloves—are superfeminine and make the bride look taller.

Short with a Few Pounds to Spare: Try a blouson bodice over a fitted slip, with a long, narrow sleeve. (Avoid the billowy look. Try a boatneck, high, or natural neckline. Gathered or slightly dirndl waists with soft ribbon accents add length. Avoid flounced skirts, and choose a delicate headpiece such as a silk-flower wreath.

Average Height, Weight: We envy you. Whether you like Victorian, traditional, or today's trendsetters (minis, tea-lengths, bubble skirts), anything will look great on you.

Tall and Thin: Dropped waists look dynamite. They take away from that long, leggy look. Bare, off-the-shoulder styles are sexy and feminine. Dramatic veilings and hats are lovely. You can handle tiers of ruffles, billowy sleeves.

Tall/Average Weight or Frame: Try a princess-style fitted bodice with some roundness to the skirt and bishop sleeves. Ankle-length, long, or scalloped hems are good.

Heavyset: Choose simple lines. Avoid too much lace or beading. Look for vertical lines such as the princess cut, a soft bodice, and natural or high necklines. Avoid very puffed sleeves, but try a dolman effect. Again, a simple headpiece, a silk-flower wreath, or a chapel veil is pretty.

   Various necklines and different waist, sleeve, and skirt treatments can change your appearance dramatically and create wonderful illusions for the less than perfect figure. While you are trying to decide what will look best on you, it helps to become familiar with some of the styles and cuts typically available in wedding gowns. (See illustrations on the following pages.)
   You should also be aware that bridal gowns come in many lengths, with or without trains. Floor-length dresses with trains have one of three types:

> *sweep length:*   falls about six inches on the floor
> *chapel length:*   falls anywhere up to twenty-two inches on the floor
> *cathedral length:*   falls beyond twenty-two inches on the floor

Within those types, there are different styles. The most popular style is the *attached* train, which simply falls from the back end of the skirt. Then there are: the *Watteau* train, which falls from the back yoke; the *capelet* train, which flows from the back shoulder; and the *detachable* train, which begins at the waistline. Don't let concern about dancing and maneuverability at the reception worry you when selecting your dress. At your final fitting, ask your bridal consultant to show you how to bustle your train so the detail will be visible, but so you can also be comfortable throughout the festivities. The same is true for a long veil, which can be tacked up under the headpiece.

Finally, there are the issues of color and fabric. Don't be misled into thinking that white is white and that all bridal fabrics are alike. There are many different whites and off-whites, each with its own tonal shadings of blue, gray, yellow, or rose. You want the shade that will best complement your particular complexion and coloration.

Fabrics too can reflect light (satins, taffetas, high-sheen silks) or add bulk (satins, velvets, nets). Each fabric has different draping and shaping capabilities. Fabrics also come in various weights; for greatest comfort, choose a weight appropriate to the season. Some wrinkle, some float, some are fragile. It pays to be aware of a fabric's properties so you can be sure that it is what works best for you. (See the "Bridal Fabric Reference Guide" page 116 .)

With the increased popularity of the romantic, formal look, there is a renewed interest in the antique or heirloom gowns. Some brides dream of wearing their mother's or grandmother's dress while others shop antique markets and clothing boutiques in search of a unique look from another era. The antique gown is a lovely tradition, but not one without its special problems. Unless the gown has been unusually well-preserved and unless it already fits fairly well, it will need to be refashioned or refurbished. And this can be a costly and difficult task.

If you are considering an antique or heirloom gown, get the knowledgeable advice of an expert seamstress or bridal consultant. Some laces and fabrics are especially hard to match, and older gowns may be too fragile to withstand reworking. Only an expert can tell you what is possible and what it will entail.

Some brides may also consider borrowing a gown, not necessarily an antique one, from a friend or relative. Again, it's the look and the fit that count. If the gown is perfect as is, then it may not be a bad idea. But if it needs reworking or refitting, the owner of the gown may quite understandably be reluctant. You should also consider the very special attachment most women have to their wedding dresses. Might you be sorry you don't own the dress when you have to give it back, or might the original owner regret that she gave her dress away? You'll have to be both sensible and sensitive if you plan to wear someone else's wedding gown. With all this discussion of traditional wedding gowns, let us not forget that many brides choose suits, cocktail dresses, or designer creations from department stores and boutiques. Except for the possibility of a guest showing up in the same dress, there is nothing wrong with this. Indeed, the formal, traditional wedding gown could be totally wrong for some weddings. Just remember, though, that only at your *own* wedding do you have the prerogative to look like a bride.

In recognition of that fact, we must also acknowledge that the traditional wedding gown is no longer the exclusive reserve of young, first-time brides. Older women, even those who have been married before, often seize the opportunity to enjoy the dress of their dreams. Ultimately, only you can determine what's right for you.

Bridal Fabric Reference Chart

When you start to shop for bridal gowns and attendants' attire, you will hear many descriptions of fabrics and trims. Use this reference guide to familiarize yourself with some of the most common bridal gown constructions. In general, you can count on natural fibers (silks, linens, and imported cottons) and handmade laces to be more expensive than synthetics.

BRIDAL FABRICS

Batistes, Voiles, Eyelets, Piqués
These are young, summery fabrics of cotton or cotton-polyester blends. Usually pure white and perfect for country and garden weddings.

Brocades, Jacquards
Natural or man-made fabrics with an embossed pattern. Have a more wintery feeling, but much depends on the styling.

Charmeuse
The classic charmeuse is made of silk, but polyester blends are also available. This soft, lightweight cloth drapes beautifully and achieves a very sophisticated look.

Chiffon
Could be an expensive silk chiffon or a less expensive polyester-silk blend. Has a floaty feeling, most often designed in layers. Very feminine and romantic.

Crepe
In polyester or rayon, heavy or lightweight, crepe has a marvelous drape for cowl necklines, raglan sleeves, and other sophisticated effects.

Crepe de chine
A silk or blended fabric with a soft, floating look most often used for informal bridals.

English net	Quality cotton net usually appliquéd with lace or left sheer at necklines for a bare yet covered look.
Faille	In pure silk or less expensive polyester, a ribbed, full-bodied fabric for high-fashion silhouettes. Wintery in feeling.
Jersey	Available both in silk jersey and in a variety of blends, this fabric has a fluid drape and can be matte or lustered.
Linen	Usually a blend to prevent excess wrinkling. This is traditionally a warm-weather fabric for constructed design.
Organza	In expensive silk or less expensive polyester blends, organza has a crisp yet sheer look and is often appliquéd.
Peau de soie	A silk blend that holds its shape for constructed designs yet has a soft, rich feel.
Satin	A beautiful, traditional bridal fabric available in silk-face (expensive) as well as blends (less costly). Some have a high gleam, but delustered versions are also available.
Taffeta	Another fabric available in silk as well as silk blends. Once a winter favorite, taffeta is now popular year-round in tissue weight. Nice body and wonderful rustle.
Tulle	The appearance of veiling. Romantic when used layer on layer, like a ballerina dress.
Velvet	Choose only cotton or polyester velvet. Some blends lack body and richness. Sophisticated fabric for winter weddings usually fashioned in simple styles with "important" trims.

LACES AND EMBROIDERIES

Alençon lace

From France, Alençon is a delicate lace available mostly in floral and leaf patterns. Reembroidery (with a corded look) defines the pattern and adds dimension. A costly lace found on better gowns.

Brussels lace

From Belgium, a rare lace, very delicate. The patterns are wispy and subtle, the threads very fine. Expensive lace of limited availability found on fine gowns.

Chantilly lace

Another French lace, soft to the touch and web-like in pattern. Authentic Chantilly is costly, but it is often copied less expensively. (Know the copy by its stiffer, heavier feel.)

Embroidered organza

Originating in Switzerland, this fabric has dimensional flowers with rolled edges appliquéd to it. Very interesting patterns with a youthful look; less traditional, more unusual than some other laces.

Schiffli embroidery

A product of the United States, Schiffli is available in intricate, delicate patterns resembling Brussels and Chantilly laces, but costs far less. Rather than a separate lace sewn to the fabric, Schiffli is design embroidered directly onto the gown.

Venise lace

Originating in Italy, Venise is a heavier lace, very dimensional, most often in leaf and floral designs. In cotton or linen it has a summery feeling, but can be worn year-round.

POPULAR WEDDING GOWN STYLES

Victorian

Sophisticated informal

Ballerina

Princess

SLEEVE STYLES

Dolman sleeve

Leg of mutton sleeve

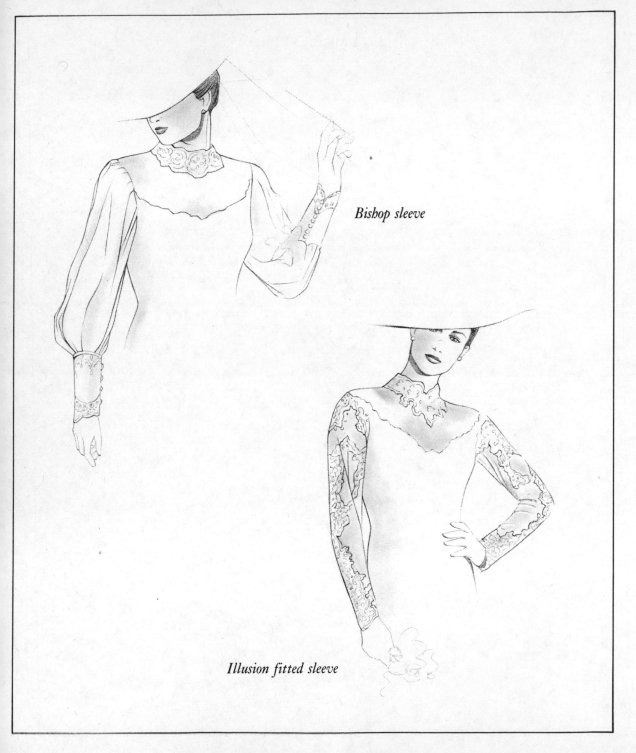

Bishop sleeve

Illusion fitted sleeve

BODICES AND WAISTLINES

Peplum bodice

Basque waist

Blouson bodice

Empire bodice

Fitted bodice, natural waist

NECKLINES

Sabrina neck

Scooped neck

Queen Anne neck

Sweetheart neck

Bateau neck

Jacqueline McCord Leo, fashion editor of *Modern Bride*, summarizes with these tips on wedding attire:

> Do your homework and know what's out there. It's a brand-new world of styles, shapes, fabrics, and silhouettes that go well beyond designer blue jeans. Once you know the choices available, stick with a style that works for the kind of wedding you're having. A gown with a cathedral train and gobs and gobs of lace would hardly work for a wedding breakfast with twenty-five guests!

Jackie adds that it's smart to remain flexible when trying on gowns at the bridal salon. You never know how much a dress may become you unless you try it on. (With wedding dresses especially, you can't tell what it really looks like when it's on the hanger.) "However, don't drive your salesperson crazy with indecision," she cautions. "A little discretion is the better part of wedding valor."

Bridal Headpieces

Whether your look is Edwardian, Victorian, Southern Belle, or "Thoroughly Modern Millie," the bridal headpice is the pièce de résistance of the ensemble and the finishing touch that distinguishes you as the bride. The hat, veil, or wreath must be chosen with your total look in mind and must do its utmost to enhance both your gown and your features.

Headpieces with veils or lace mantillas are the traditional bridal choices, while picture hats, floral wreaths, or ribbon cascades are more contemporary options. The latter work best with informal and sophisticated gowns, the more traditional headpieces with more classic attire.

Veils may be long or short, falling anywhere from the shoulder to the floor, and are usually made of nylon or silk. The fine netting of these fabrics creates the illusion effect, a cloud-like fantasy look, and allows them to be used in multiple layers and different shapings. Veiling may even be appliquéd with lace, giving it a look similar to the all-lace mantilla.

Veiling is anchored to a small hat or headpiece designed to sit on the crown of the head. It may be just basted to the headpiece for easy removal later. You'll want to keep the activities of your ceremony and reception in mind when considering veil lengths and headpiece constructions.

Wedding hats, with or without veiling, come in every conceivable size and shape. Small hats such as turbans or pillboxes are often chosen for a more sophisticated look, work well with almost any hairstyle, and complement the more tailored gown or suit. Large-brimmed hats, on the other hand, make a much more dramatic statement and render something of a costume effect. They are usually expensive and are not appropriate for every woman and every wedding style. Several of the most popular headpiece styles are illustrated on pages 127–128).

HEADPIECES

Hat

Wreath

Mantilla

Tiara

Floral wreaths, combs, or ribbon cascades, all with or without veiling, are popular among brides who prefer a simpler, more understated look. Such headpieces are often fashioned of fresh or silk flowers, or embellished with pearls or lace.

Whatever your style, give careful attention to the selection of your bridal headpiece. Here are some pointers:

1. When shopping for a headpiece, wear your hair the way you plan to on your wedding day.
2. Try on your selection with your gown (if not available, with a gown of equivalent styling) to get the overall effect.
3. Think about lighting and photography. Does your headpiece obscure your facial features?
4. Discuss with your salesperson how you want to look after the ceremony. Is your headpiece conducive to hugging, kissing, or dancing?
5. Make sure your headpiece is comfortable and can be firmly attached to your head.

Accessories

"Something old, something new, something borrowed, something blue . . ." Whether it is an antique lace handkerchief or a stunning new strand of pearls from the groom, you'll probably want to incorporate this age-old bridal tradition into your choice of wedding accessories. Jewelry, shoes, gloves, flowers, heirlooms— all make up the list of accessory possibilities. You just have to choose tastefully.

In general, jewelry should be unobtrusive and should complement the neckline of your gown and the styling of your hair and headpiece. Pearls, lockets, or small chains for neckware; pearl, diamond, or gold earrings; and perhaps a dainty bracelet are the usual choices. Large, dramatic jewelry is appropriate for only the most sophisticated ensemble.

If you're wearing gloves over the elbow, remember that you will be receiving a ring. With long gloves, you can have the seams of the ring finger opened for this occasion and resewn later. Otherwise, you don't want to carry or wear anything that you cannot gracefully transfer to an attendant during the ceremony. Keep that in mind when choosing your floral bouquet, too. (See "Flowers," page 140.)

When it comes to shoes, consider both style and comfort. A bride whose feet are killing her will not get the most enjoyment out of her special day. Shoes can be sandals or pumps, fabric or leather, whatever is suitable to the style of your dress. Just be sure that they fit properly and that you can walk gracefully in them. Bridal shops generally have a selection of shoes, but regular shoe outlets may also carry suitable styles, possibly at lower prices, particularly in the spring and summer when white and light shoes are in stock.

Hose can be white or light, patterned or plain, as you wish—except if your shoes are lacy, in which case your hose should be plain.

Bibles, rosaries, fans, baskets, parasols, walking canes, and heaven knows what else have been carried by brides over the years. If you have a sound religious or sentimental reason for carrying an object down the aisle, then do so. But if you are doing it just for effect, then maybe you ought to rethink your motivation. The traditional bouquet is usually a bride's most suitable adornment.

Underpinnings

To quote from Erma Bombeck, "Anything that has a new beginning is given status by new underwear. For instance, I have never known anyone personally who would consider marriage without buying new undergarments for each day of the honeymoon."[1] She's right, of course. But over and above the importance of new beginnings is the importance of underpinnings as the unsung, unseen heroes of the perfect bridal look. The appropriate bridal lingerie provides stiffness or puffiness where required (under a flounced skirt, for example) and is invisible everywhere else. The salesperson or bridal consultant who sells you your gown can tell you exactly what you need underneath to make your wedding finery look just right.

Bridal Trousseau

Today's practical, cost-conscious women recognize that a bridal trousseau is much more than just a honeymoon wardrobe. Certainly the honeymoon destination may necessitate some particular purchases geared to anticipated climates or activities— a new swimsuit, tennis togs, or the like. But over and above honeymoon considerations, you'll want your trousseau to help fill the business, social, and at-home needs of your life as a newlywed.

More than likely you have already developed your own fashion sense. Shopping for your trousseau offers you the opportunity to fill in basic wardrobe items that will coordinate with what you already own, as well as the excuse to splurge on some extras that will expand and enhance your clothing selection.

For most brides, the splurge comes in lingerie. The exciting array of sensuous fabrics, alluring designs, and luscious colors has made the white peignoir all but passé. Indulge yourself. This is probably the one time in life when you can justify buying lots of new undergarments.

When shopping for your trousseau, look for easy-care items. The wonderful combinations of natural and synthetic fibers used by most manufacturers mean that no new bride should have to spend hours at the ironing board (though she may have to make trips to the cleaners now and then to assure proper care of silks and other fine fabrics).

A beautiful trousseau is a bridal prerogative, but it can be as practical as it is pretty. Enjoy!

Male Attire

The groom's choice of formalwear for himself and his groomsmen is determined by the degree of formality of the wedding, the time of day, and the color of the gowns selected by the bride for her attendants. (See "What To Wear," page 132.) For men, there are two ways to go: either with traditional, classic formalwear or with the more contemporary formal suits, which are adaptations of the classics.

For daytime, the classics include the morning suit—a gray or black stroller with striped trouser and striped four-in-hand tie—or the cutaway (what all the presidents wear on Inauguration Day). After 6:00 P.M., the attire may be black tie, which means the traditional all-black tuxedo—black tie, black jacket and pants, optional accessories—or simply formal, meaning a white dinner jacket with black trousers in summer, or the velvet or silk smoker with black trousers in winter.

The ultimate in classic evening attire is Fred Astaire's favorite, white tie and tails. This is the black tailcoat with all-white piqué accessories and a wing-collared shirt. It is the most formal, elegant attire a man can wear, and is reserved for only the most formal, elegant affairs, usually of three hundred guests or more.

While the outfits named above form the proper core of men's formalwear, the classic choices have been creatively adapted into a whole spectrum of contemporary formal suits. Colorful jackets over traditional black trousers or matching jackets or tailcoats and trousers in white, gray, brown, or other shades serve as good coordinates to attendants' dresses and move gracefully from day into evening.

When you and your fiancé discuss male attire, think in terms of classic or contemporary. Consider the look of the whole wedding in making your decision. If you choose to go with one of the classic styles, then don't deviate from its requirements. The fact that an ascot always demands a wing collar or that a four-in-hand takes a tab collar may seem like trivial bits of information, but having all the correct elements is crucial to the propriety of the classic style. You may adapt the rules, if this is your preference, but choose a definite contemporary look. Don't make the mistake of simply mismatching classic attire. Instead, choose the outfit and accessories with an eye for updated, tastefully untraditional styling to create a harmonious ensemble. Your formalwear specialist can give you expert guidance concerning what's available along contemporary lines.

What to Wear

The size of the wedding, the time of day, the location, and the formality of the bride's
dress are what determine the style of the wedding. This chart is a guide to assist you with

TYPE OF WEDDING	BRIDE	BRIDESMAIDS
Formal Daytime	White, ivory, or delicate pastel tinted floor-length wedding dress with a cathedral or chapel (sweep) train. Long veil covering the train or making the train. If shorter, then very full with many layers. Bouquet or prayer book; shoes to match gown; long gloves with short sleeves, otherwise gloves are optional; simple jewelry.	Floor-length dresses, simple cap or hat, with or without a short veil; gloves to complement the length of sleeves; shoes to match or blend with dresses; any style bouquet; honor attendant's dress may match or contrast in colors with other attendants' dresses.
Formal Evening	Six o'clock is the hour that separates the formal evening wedding from the formal day wedding. Wedding dress is the same as for the daytime, sleeves should be long. Fabrics may be more elaborate.	Long evening dresses; accessories same as daytime. Fabrics can be more elaborate.

everyone's attire, but it is always subject to changes in fashion. For example, styles in menswear have become more versatile. Local formalwear specialists throughout the country can advise you on the newest choices for rental or purchase. Your personal preferences guided by your bridal consultant's advice will help you plan a beautiful wedding. In a second marriage, the bride should feel free to follow her wishes and white is a valid choice.

MOTHERS	MEN
Simple floor-length or three-quarter-length dress, small hats (optional), shoes, gloves, and corsage to harmonize. The mothers' ensembles should complement each other in regard to style, color, and length.	**Traditional:** cutaway coat (either oxford gray or black) with striped trousers, gray waistcoat, wing-collared white shirt, and a striped ascot. **Contemporary:** black or gray contoured long or short jacket, striped trousers, wing-collared white shirt; gray vest (optional). Same style jacket in selection of colors, matching pants, and coordinated shirt.
Floor-length evening dresses, small head covering; dressy accessories—furs; jewelry.	**Traditional:** after 6.00 P.M., tails, matching trousers, waistcoat, wing-collared shirt, bow tie. Ultraformal: black tails, white tie. **Contemporary:** contoured long or short jacket, matching trousers, wing-collared shirt; vest or cummerbund, bow tie.

TYPE OF WEDDING	BRIDE	BRIDESMAIDS
Semiformal Daytime	White or pastel floor-length dress. Veil: elbow length or shorter. Same accessories as formal wedding.	Same as for formal wedding, although cut and fabrics may be simpler.
Semiformal Evening	Same as daytime. Fabrics or trim may be more elaborate.	Long evening dresses; accessories same as daytime. Fabrics may be more elaborate.
Informal Daytime and Evening	White or pastel floor-length dress, or short dress, or suit. Short veil or bridal-type hat. Small bouquet, corsage, or prayer book. Suitable gloves and complementary shoes.	Same length dress as bride wears; however, if bride wears floor-length style, it is permissible for attendant to wear a short dress. Accessories should be simple and suitable to the ensemble.
Guests	At a formal wedding, women wear street-length dresses or suits in the daytime, long dresses in the evening, and the	

MOTHERS	MEN
Same as for formal wedding.	**Traditional:** gray or black stroller, striped trousers, gray vest, white soft-collared shirt, gray and white striped tie. **Contemporary:** formal suit in a choice of colors and styles, matching or contrasting trousers, white or colored shirt. Bow tie, vest, or cummerbund.
Same as for formal wedding.	**Traditional:** black dinner jacket, matching trousers, black vest or cummerbund, white dress shirt, black bow tie. In warm weather, white or ivory jacket. **Contemporary:** formal suit (darker shades for fall and winter, lighter shades for spring and summer); matching or contrasting trousers. Bow tie to match vest or cummerbund.
Street-length dress or suit ensemble.	Black, dark gray, or navy business suit. In summer, white or natural-colored jacket, dark tropical worsted trousers, navy jacket, white flannel trousers, or white suit.

attire for men is coordinated to their escorts, unless otherwise stated on the invitation.

TRADITIONAL MENSWEAR STYLES

White tie

Formal

Black tie

Cutaway

Morning suit

As soon as the groom knows the date of the wedding and the bride-to-be has selected her bridesmaids' dresses, the groom should contact his local specialist to select his formalwear. The specialist should be provided with measurements (jacket size, inseam, waist, and shirt size) for all out-of-town attendants. Ideally the final fitting should be done several days in advance. If only one or two of the men are not available until the day before, alert your formalwear shop and they will do their best to accommodate you.

Formal rentals will run about $60, not including shoes. The groom and grooms-men generally dress alike, with only a different boutonniere to distinguish the man of the hour. If your beloved wants to make more of a fashion statement, advise him to do it in a subtle way, perhaps with a colored cummerbund or other ac-cessories.

Fathers wear the same or similar attire, though if the wedding is black-tie and one of them owns his own tuxedo, it is advisable to let him wear it. (Generally, the same is true of other members of the wedding party as well.) If the wedding is semiformal or informal, a dark suit or blazer will also do, and the men in the wedding party do not have to be dressed identically, but comparably.

A final note. Nothing looks worse with elegant formalwear than scruffy, informal footwear. Make sure that each attendant has the appropriate shoes for his outfit, or plan to have them rent shoes from the formalwear specialist.

Bridesmaids' Attire

Have a heart! Unless you are uncommonly wealthy or generous, bridesmaids will probably be paying for their own outfits, in addition to any other expenses your wedding causes them to incur. Thus they deserve to have their individual styles and figures as well as their budgets considered in the choice, and probably secretly hope you'll have the good sense to pick a dress they can wear more than once.

Happily, manufacturers of attendants attire recognize those needs and have sup-plied an infinite selection of gowns in generally moderate price ranges. You can find cocktail dresses coordinated with discreet cover-ups, tiered skirts that can be worn long or short, tunics, and camisoles. You can purchase one style in many colors, or one color in many styles. You can even find more youthful renditions of the same outfit for junior bridesmaids and flower girls.

With so much to choose from in so broad a price range, there is really no reason to saddle any woman in your wedding party with an outfit that doesn't become her. Once you have decided on the general tone of your wedding and the degree of formality, discuss your ideas and preferences with your attendants. You might even ask them to drop by the bridal salon to look over some styles or colors you're considering. The very fact that they have agreed to be a part of your wedding ensures their willingness to cooperate if asked.

Nobody has a better selection than the bridal shops. However, if you wish, you can also check department stores and boutiques. Again, refer to "What to Wear" (page 132) for guidance in style selection.

Color is a matter of very personal preference. Usually, lighter colors are worn in spring and summer, more vibrant tones in fall and winter. Even the all-white wedding is enjoying renewed popularity. To achieve a coordinated effect, you will want to consider accent colors you might use throughout the wedding in floral arrangements, table settings, cake decorations, and so forth. A monochromatic scheme of differing hues of the same color can be very pleasing, and can offer shade variations suitable for every person and every thing.

Accessories provide a good opportunity to combine your bridesmaids' gifts with what they will need that day. Gloves, jewelry, or hair ornaments can be chosen to accent the look of the dress while supplying a welcome remembrance for your attendants.

You may or may not want to distinguish your maid/matron of honor. If you do, it can be done with flowers and accessories or with a different shade of dress (for example, light pink for the maid of honor, deeper pink for the other maids).

When your wedding is small, with only an honor attendant and perhaps one other, it is probably best to let her (them) select and coordinate the gown(s), as long as you're satisfied that their dresses will complement the overall style of the wedding.

Mothers' Attire

The mother of the bride and the mother of the groom wear the same length gown or suit, long or short, depending on the formality of the wedding. According to strictest protocol, the bride's mother chooses what she will wear first, then informs the groom's mother so she can make a selection suitable in color and length. The idea was that one mother, especially the groom's, should not outshine the other.

Such rigid protocol is rarely employed anymore. While the mothers should agree on the degree of formality, each should have her own prerogative in style and color. Sometimes a mother may even choose to wear an appropriate dress she already owns.

If the bridal couple is fortunate enough to have their proud grandmothers in attendance, the bride, her mother, and her future mother-in-law can help these very special ladies choose their outfits for this very special day. Wedding consultants and sales personnel in the bridal shops and in the bridal department of local stores will happily give you as much time as you require to help outfit all your VIPs.

Completing the Picture

No doubt when you visualize your ideal wedding, you think in terms of a perfect setting, a pervasive mood. But a setting can have many different moods, depending on how it is enhanced. All the elements that complete the wedding picture—the flowers, the music, the services—must be carefully chosen to provide just the right environment for the kind of wedding you imagine. With all wedding-related services, the best recommendation you can get concerning the quality of work is through word of mouth. Satisfied customers are the most reliable reference.

Flowers

Flowers are like makeup: they should beautify the whole without drawing undue notice to themselves. Most brides rightly recognize the importance of their floral selections to the overall style of their wedding. But they may not be aware of the time and expertise required of a floral designer to achieve a harmonious effect.

Once you have determined the degree of formality of your wedding and have selected your own gown and the attendants' attire, you will want to consult a florist. Four to six months in advance is not too early for busy, popular florists. You will want to bring a colored fabric swatch and, if possible, a sketch or photograph of your dress with you. Be prepared to discuss the ceremony and reception sites in some detail, and have an idea of the number and types of arrangements you will need.

Flowers in season are always less expensive, but you may have a special look or theme requiring the unusual. Silk flowers are another option. You may not want to incur the expense of all silk, but they do work very well in combination with fresh or dried flowers. Should you be contemplating complete silk arrangements for yourself or your attendants, it may help to know that florists can rearrange bouquets into permanent arrangements after the wedding. They become lasting mementos that may make the cost worthwhile.

Compare estimates from more than one florist and be certain your commitment is accompanied by a written agreement. Most bouquets and arrangements are composed of flowers, fillers, and greenery, so you'll want to be sure you know just how much and what kind of each you're paying for.

Year-round traditional favorites include stephanotis, delphiniums, carnations, roses, mums, and some orchid varieties. These flowers are popular because they combine well with other varieties and are durable. Let your florist advise you on what's in season and what special properties certain flowers have.

If you're on a tight budget, you don't have to limit your choices to cut flowers. You can also rent or buy potted plants, flowers, and trees. Some florists even rent silk arrangements. You might also consider sharing floral arrangements with another bride getting married the same day. Remember too that in the church or temple elaborate flowers are appropriate only at the largest, most formal weddings. Usually a nice altar arrangement and perhaps some simple pew markers will suffice.

In the Jewish wedding the chuppah is sometimes made entirely of flowers. (See "The Jewish Wedding," page 86.) This expense can also be limited by using a combination of flowers and greenery.

If your wedding reception is strictly a stand-up affair, then you will need only an arrangement or two and perhaps a table garland. If, however, your reception is a sit-down dinner, then you will want to plan for table centerpieces and a more elaborate arrangement at the main table. There may be other extras: stanchions, decorations for the wedding cup or cake knife and for the bridal book, even flowers in the ladies' room!

Centerpieces can be as simple or as elaborate as you like. Just be sure they are not so large or high as to obstruct service or conversation. Whatever is chosen should be consistent with the colors and style used during the ceremony and should not clash with the existing decor of the reception site.

During holidays it may not be necessary to invest in elaborate floral decorations, as one bride found to her most pleasant surprise. The country inn at which she was having her dinner reception two days after Christmas was already fully decorated with wreaths, Yule logs, fireplace garlands, and centerpieces of poinsettias. They simply had no more room for flowers of any kind! (The same is true during Eastertime and other celebrations throughout the year.) Think about it . . .

Before you make any specific selections, be sure to check with personnel at the site(s) of your ceremony and reception. Do fire laws prohibit the use of candles and sconces? Must flowers be in keeping with the colors of the liturgical season? Is a wedding runner or carpet available, or must you secure one? Can floral deliveries be made directly to the site? If so, when, and who will receive them? You will need to be sure of all facts and aware of any restrictions before giving instructions to the florist. (If the florist is already familiar with the site(s), you will have to go no further for the information.)

Bouquets and Boutonnieres

Regardless of the type of wedding you have, you will probably carry a bridal bouquet. This tradition has endured because bridal flowers symbolize the love and joy of the occasion.

Choose your bouquet to complement you and your dress. There are several standard shapes (see the illustrations), but almost anything is possible. The size of your bouquet should be in proportion to your height and dress style. Big, voluminous bouquets may be in fashion, but as pretty as flowers are, you don't want to be hidden behind them! A good florist can provide valuable advice about the type of arrangement that will suit you best.

BOUQUETS

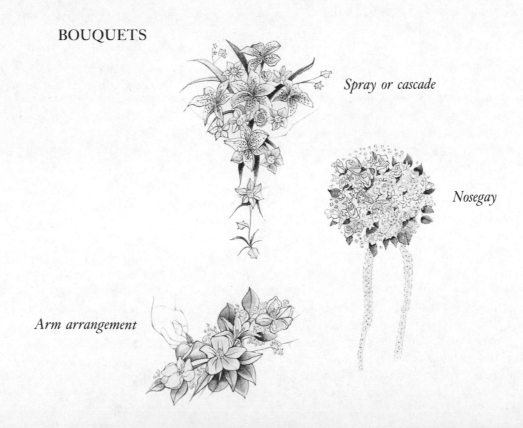

Spray or cascade

Nosegay

Arm arrangement

You may wish to have something special worked into your bouquet—a prayer book or rosary, for example. Again, your florist can advise you concerning what is appropriate and how it can be done.

Bridal bouquets do not have to be white, though white usually dominates. Nor, as already mentioned, do they have to consist of all fresh flowers. Even a single beautiful blossom like a dramatic orchid or a long-stemmed rose enhanced with ribbon or lace can be striking.

Keep in mind that there are many ways your bouquet can be fashioned. Inquire about having your flowers made into a breakaway bouquet; the concealed center (or bottom tail if it's a cascade) is removable. After you've tossed the bouquet, you'll still have a corsage for the honeymoon and a keepsake from your special day.

Bridesmaids' bouquets should complement your own in color and type but need not match yours in the style in which they are fashioned. The same considerations of individual size and dress proportions are important in their selection.

If you want to distinguish your maid/matron of honor and make her feel special, say it with flowers. Use different ribbons or a different color combination, and make her bouquet a cross between your own and those of the bridesmaids.

If you're planning on having flower girls, consider their size and youth when selecting their bouquets. The most fragile blossoms will never hold up. Small basket arrangements or miniature nosegays are in proportion, more durable, and very charming.

A boutonniere delivers the finishing touch to any man's tuxedo lapel. The ushers usually wear a carnation, but the groom's boutonniere is traditionally taken from a flower in the bride's bouquet. While almost any flower can be used for a boutonniere, many grooms today wear a rose, stephanotis, or cymbidium orchid for very formal weddings. Discuss this with your florist to make the wisest selection.

No flower is wilt-proof, but some last better than others. Stephanotis and freesia are still popular for this reason. One tip all florists offer is that you keep all the wedding party flowers in the refrigerator until the last possible moment; they'll stay fresh much longer.

Mothers and grandmothers can wear their corsages on the bodice, at the waist, on the wrist, or attached to a handbag. While the groom traditionally pays for these flowers (as well as for the bridal bouquet and the boutonnieres), it is probably best to order them when ordering for all the rest of the wedding party. It's nice if the mothers' corsages can be somewhat in keeping with other wedding flowers, but their own preferences and dress selections should be the prime consideration.

Reception Music

Music for the reception is quite another matter from music for the ceremony. If you are having a brunch or lunch or something approaching an afternoon tea, soft background music provided by a pianist, harpist, or string quartet might be just the right touch. If, on the other hand, you have something more lively in mind, then you'll want to begin making inquiries of your favorite bands, combos, and DJs several months in advance. Whatever type of musical accompaniment you choose, be sure it's something you and your guests will enjoy.

Most major caterers and hotels have affiliated musicians whom you can employ for your reception. Just be sure you've heard them and that you like them. Musicians are paid by the hour according to union scale, and their contracts include set playing limits and so many breaks per hour. If you'd like continuous music, check on the extra cost. It might be worth it.

DJs for the reception are growing in popularity, not only because they are often less expensive (fees start at around $200) but also because they can usually arrange to provide varied and continuous entertainment. As you know from listening to your favorite radio station, a disc jockey's personality is of prime importance. So you'll want to be sure the style of the DJ you are considering is suitable for your needs.

When arranging the contract, be sure you understand all fees and restrictions and are aware of any conditions that could result in additional charges (for example, extending into overtime, providing food and drink). Because the sound of a group may change as musicians leave and are replaced by others, you'll also want to be sure that the group you've heard and enjoyed will remain essentially the same. And don't forget to tell the musicians in advance if you will want them to play any special musical selections for which they might have to prepare (ethnic music, favorite songs, etc.).

Finally, let's not rule out the possibility of taped music for the ceremony or the reception. If employed tastefully and discreetly, taped recordings can supply much-needed atmosphere on a very limited budget. Make sure the sound system you'll be using has enough power to fill the room without a lot of distortion (you may want to rent or borrow a stereo if yours doesn't fill the bill).

By the way, if you will be using your own piano or organ at home, be sure it has been properly tuned.

Photographs

Couples often underestimate the worth and overestimate the expense of professional wedding photography. According to marketing research by the Eastman Kodak Company, a scant 45 percent of wedding pictures are done by professional photographers.[2]

Frankly, many couples are missing out. It's great to have talented friends and family members take photos of your special day, and granted, some of their shots may be quite good—when their attention isn't diverted by the festivities or their equipment isn't malfunctioning. But only an experienced, objective professional can guarantee to capture the memories of a lifetime in print.

Obviously, some professional photographers are better than others. Some are more creative, some have better equipment, some are more experienced, some have more sophisticated lab facilities. Nevertheless, when you consider the time, energy, and expertise you're getting for between $300 and $1000, it seems to be money well spent.

You'll want to interview several photographers so as to get an idea of their individual styles and price structures. Most wedding specialists offer packages that may include your formal portrait, coverage of the wedding day, a bridal album of so many prints, and smaller albums or collections for the parents. Again, beware of any unbelievable deals. One New York bride is still waiting to see pictures from her wedding of two years ago!

Standard contracts define the number and sizes of prints (from proofs) you will receive, any special albums or mountings, the delivery dates of proofs and prints, the rights to negatives, and specified rates for additional prints and services. Make sure your photographer is familiar with the site(s) he'll be working in, and that someone will be available the day of the wedding to point out key individuals.

Above all, don't be shy about spelling out exactly what you want. The more information you can give the photographer, the more adeptly he can do his job. Here are some questions to think about:

- Do you want portrait (posed) shots or candid shots or both?
- Are there any special people or problems he should be aware of?
- Are there restrictions concerning when and where pictures can be taken in your church or synagogue? (Check with the clergy.)
- Will he have to work around any other professionals—a videotaping crew, for example—that day?
- If you do not own the negatives, how long will they be available for reprints?
- What are the exact date(s), times, and places you'll expect him to be on hand?

Videotape Recordings

Videotape has become the newest technological innovation for the wedding day. It is so new, in fact, that it may not be readily available in all areas. But if you truly want this very special day recorded in sound and action, it may be worth investigating. The following general information will help you decide whether or not to pursue the possibility.

First, it takes money—at least $500 for a two-hour tape, probably a good bit more. As with any production, you will have to be sure of the talents of your camera operator and crew and willing to devote some of your own time to the planning, staging, and editing of the footage.

There are a variety of approaches to filming. Your wedding day can be done as a news narrative with a commentator, as a romantic tale with music and flashbacks, or as a real-life drama with close-ups and candids. Just be aware that moving equipment, changing locations, and editing in extras will add to overall production costs.

There is no question that the presence of a crew with lights, cameras, and sound equipment will create excitement, especially if you have a still-life photographer on the premises as well. You'll need to consider how this will affect the mood of your wedding, and find out if the cleric has any objections. Videotaping does not have to be disruptive if the cameras and crew are more or less stationary.

Talk about all of this with your video specialist. Make sure that you see samples of his work, that you understand all the terms of the agreement, and that he is aware of any special requirements or restrictions. Then after the wedding sit back with a glass of champagne and enjoy the show again and again!

Transportation

You can get to the church on time in anything from a gleaming white stretch limousine to a double-decker bus. You can hire a classic car, a horse and buggy, or an old-fashioned sleigh. Or you can simply settle for the family station wagon.

In short, it doesn't really matter what *kind* of transportation you have as long as you *have* some. Consider the alternatives: misplaced people, hefty traffic tickets, full parking lots. A few prior arrangements can alleviate the threat of mishap.

If your wedding is of any size at all, you'll probably want to notify your local police department. They can issue variances for curb-side parking and can also provide the names of off-duty officers you can employ to monitor especially difficult parking or traffic situations (in crowded cities or private neighborhoods, for instance).

If you're using private cars, make sure that all the members of the wedding party are assigned to certain vehicles, that they know what time they are to arrive for the ceremony, and that the cars are lined up out front to transport the wedding party promptly to the reception. (Be sure to write a note of thanks to any individual who provides his car and services that day.)

Going to the ceremony, your mother and honor attendant traditionally ride in the first car, the other maids in the second, and you and your father in the third. You may also wish to make special arrangements for the groom's parents. (The groom and the ushers arrange for their own transportation; usually the best man is responsible for making the arrangements.) Leaving the ceremony, you and the groom are in the first car, your parents in the next, and your attendants (male and female) in the others.

The same arrangements are made if you are using a hired service. Limousines charge flat rates that vary from region to region but usually include the driver's tip. (Check to be sure; if not, 15 percent is customary.) See the Yellow Pages for services in your area.

If you anticipate any problems in guest parking, check with your reception manager and/or the police department. If you are using a garage or other limited facilities, you may have to at least look into the possibility of reserving space. You should prepay any parking fees guests might incur.

Out-of-town guests without cars pose another problem. Avail yourself of local friends who may have offered to help. They can make things easier for visitors.

Transportation planning may involve some time and trouble you'd like to avoid, but your guests will appreciate your thoughtfulness. Moreover, your efforts will contribute to the smooth flow of your wedding-day activities.

Out-of-Town Accommodations

Today families and friends are often dispersed in faraway places. Thus a wedding will often precipitate a gathering of the clan from around the world. When the out-of-towners will include members of the families and the wedding party, they deserve some special attention.

No one expects you to pay for their travel expenses, but you *can* make their travel less of a hassle. Offer to help out by providing plane, train, and local shuttle schedules. Ask area friends to help out with airport and train station pickups. One Texas bride even coordinated car-pool car rentals in Houston for members of the wedding party who couldn't fly into her hometown ninety miles away.

If you have friends who offer to house visiting guests, fine. But bear in mind that some people appreciate the excuse to get away for your wedding and may not be comfortable staying with others they hardly know. When your wedding involves a good many out-of-towners, it might be worthwhile to reserve a block of rooms at a nearby hotel. (Often you can get special rate discounts. Check on it.) Otherwise, you should at least be ready with a list of recommended convenient lodgings.

Out-of-town guests go to unusual trouble and expense to attend a wedding. Anything you can do to make them feel welcome will be appreciated. If their trip will involve a weekend or more, it's nice to plan some special social activities just for them. (See "Wedding Parties," page 150.)

To make the point, an inspirational example of the ultimate in thoughtfulness comes from a Connecticut bride. Her evening wedding was to be held in December, and she was particularly concerned about her elderly relatives and family friends on Staten Island. Would the weather cooperate? Would they be able to make the two-hour drive each way on a Saturday? Would fear keep many of them at home?

The bus she chartered to transport them may have been Trailways, but it was definitely first class all the way!

Mementos

Special mementos for the guests have gotten a lot more creative and sophisticated than the matchbooks and swizzle sticks of former years. When today's brides and grooms elect to spend money on favors, they want them to be unique remembrances that their guests can keep and enjoy.

One such item is the keepsake program. Inside an artistic cover, the details of the wedding ceremony are preserved: vows, music selections, special readings, and the names of the members of the wedding party. (Such booklets can be expanded to include the entire nuptial mass for Catholic couples.) Ask your stationer when ordering your invitations, or inquire at your church or synagogue. Wedding programs are a dignified and useful memento.

Breakaway arrangements of tiny potted flowers at the reception are lovely souvenirs. All of them together look like one large table centerpiece. But when guests leave, each can take a small plant home. Ask your florist about these.

If you can afford it, flowers offer many favor possibilities: a single blossom at each place, tiny bud vases of fresh flowers, or silk-flower napkin rings. Everybody loves floral favors, so let your imagination and budget guide you.

You can also use the theme of the season when planning wedding mementos. Ceramic eggs, Christmas ornaments, candy hearts, and the like can add to your own festivities while taking advantage of a nearby holiday.

On the more economical side, don't overlook talented friends who may be willing and able to help you design original mementos: hand-calligraphied place cards, tiny baskets or nut cups, small candles or ceramic items, decorated champagne glasses. Perhaps someone with an instant-developing camera could even take everyone's picture. With the proliferation of interest in crafts, most of us have one or two creative friends who might just be delighted to contribute his or her talents to a wedding-day celebration.

Wedding mementos are not absolutely necessary or expected, and many brides forgo them in lieu of other items. But if you can spare even a little time and money, you may be able to devise that special something through which your day can be more fondly remembered.

Groom's Cake

In some areas of the country a groom's cake is de rigueur; in others it is an elegant extra. Most commonly German chocolate or spice, it is a flat sheet cake decorated in the colors of the wedding (not white). It is either cut and served at the reception or distributed to departing guests in small individual boxes to be enjoyed later.

While we're on the subject of cake boxes, the bride's cake too is sometimes packaged and distributed for guests to take home. Single women who put bridal cake under their pillow at night will have happy dreams of their grooms-to-be, or so the legend says. Ask your caterer about cakes and boxes.

Special Touches

Individual rice bags, scented candles and flowers in the ladies' room, men's and ladies' lounge attendants, valet parking, pretty guest soaps and towels, prepaid coat check, white ribbons and bows decorating the driveway—all these thoughtful considerations indicate a flair for entertaining and a personal concern for guests.

Don't overlook the importance of the little things as valuable ingredients of your wedding style. The unexpected nicety, not necessarily expensive, adds class to any occasion and imbues it with an individual touch.

Wedding Parties

As hectic as the days preceding a wedding are, "why," you ask, "would anyone make them more so by having parties?" Quite simply, the answer is tradition. The last few days before a wedding have an air of heartfelt thank-yous, fond farewells, and the big send-off from single life. Customarily these days are spent with those closest to you, and the wedding parties given reflect that.

Understand that no one *has* to have these parties, and for very small weddings they may not even be appropriate. But more traditional weddings usually incorporate some or all of these celebrations, and many couples remember them with special fondness.

The Bridal Luncheon

This is strictly for the girls. A week or two before the wedding, the bride hosts a luncheon for her maids, her mother, and the groom's mother. Other very special female friends or relatives may also be included. The luncheon can be at your home or in a club or restaurant, and can be as formal or informal as you like. Written or phoned invitations will set the tone, and flowers and decorations enhance the festivities.

If you're not having a rehearsal dinner, then you may wish to give your bridesmaids their gifts at this luncheon. Otherwise, cute favors or sincere thank-yous will do. The important thing is that you enjoy each other's company and have a relaxing, chatty time.

Some working brides have found a luncheon difficult to arrange and have scheduled their parties in the evening. That's fine too. From foie gras to fudge sundaes, anything you and your friends enjoy is perfectly appropriate.

The Bachelor Dinner

This one is strictly for the fellows and is hosted by a close friend(s) of the groom or by the groom himself. While the bachelor dinner was traditionally intended to be a bawdy farewell to bachelorhood, most of these revelries are more benign than men would have us believe.

The bachelor party is held at a home, club, or restaurant a few days before the wedding. A good bit of drinking is the focus of the evening. At one point, the groom is supposed to raise a toast to his absent bride, and then all men smash their glasses against the fireplace so that they will never be used for a less honorable purpose. (It would be a very good idea to check with the proprietor of the place before carrying out this custom.)

If there is to be no other opportunity, the groom can give his ushers their gifts. Generally, though, conviviality and carousing are the main events. As the bride, don't nag about the details of the evening. A little feigned jealousy, however, certainly won't hurt his ego.

The Rehearsal Dinner

The rehearsal dinner follows the wedding rehearsal an evening or two before the ceremony. Even couples having small weddings that don't require a rehearsal may wish to have an intimate dinner with families and friends anyway. Invitations are mailed or phoned a couple of weeks before the wedding.

The dinner is traditionally hosted by the groom's parents at their home or at a club or restaurant, though as we've already discussed, wedding and party expenses may be handled differently. Guests include the bride and groom, the attendants and their spouses, both sets of parents, the cleric (and spouse), and any other special friends or relatives the host may wish to invite. Do make every effort to include out-of-town guests. It's a nice gesture to invite the music director or organist, the parents of flower girls or ring bearers (small children are not included), and any others who are directly involved in the wedding, but it is not absolutely necessary.

Whether in size or style, you don't want the rehearsal dinner to upstage the wedding itself. It may be quite formal and elegant, but only in proportion to the overall style of the wedding. On the other hand, it can be a backyard barbecue.

If the dinner is held the evening preceding the ceremony, you'll want to be sure guests don't end up hung over and exhausted the day of the wedding. Someone other than the host should signal an end to the evening, and the bride and groom should plan to leave before midnight.

The only real tradition of the rehearsal dinner is the toasting of the bride and groom by the best man. Other toasts—to parents, to each other, to friends—often follow. This is also an appropriate time to present your attendants with their gifts.

Attendants' Gifts

You and your fiancé are the best judges of what kinds of gifts your attendants would appreciate. Generally, all ushers' gifts and all bridesmaids' gifts are alike, while the best man and the maid/matron of honor receive something a little more special.

If you have the time and are so inclined, every gift can be different and truly personal as long as each represents approximately the same dollar value. Monogramming is another way to make each gift individual. Just be sure you shop early enough to have them ready in time.

Here are some gift ideas:

For Men

book (personally inscribed)	pen/pencil
business card case	photo album
collar stay collection	pocket calculator
credit card case	record album
cuff links	silver-plated or brass shot cup
date book	stationery
key ring	tie tack or clip
letter opener	travel kit
money clip	wallet
paperweight	

For Women

book (personally inscribed)	perfume bottle
bracelet	photo album
cosmetic bag	picture frame
date book	pocket calculator
diary	record album
earrings	scarf/handkerchief
evening bag	silver-plated comb/brush
key ring	stationery
letter opener	stickpin
paperweight	vanity set
pen/pencil	

You may also want to remember your parents with some special keepsake at this time. Whatever you choose, it should be sentimental and memorable. A hand-written letter of reflection on your lives and your relationship is a surefire hit!

The idea with all tokens is to make people feel warm and appreciated. Gifts only have to be thoughtful and personal, not expensive, to achieve that end.

Entertainment for Out-of-Town Guests

When visitors attending your wedding are staying a couple of days or more, try to plan some special activities for them while they are in town. Former friends and classmates may look forward to your wedding as an opportunity to visit with those they don't often get to see. Others may want extra time to spend with you and your future spouse.

See if you can think of fun ways to entertain out-of-towners without putting an undue burden on already busy friends and relatives. Your mother won't really appreciate a house full of company on the morning of the wedding.

If guests are to be included in the rehearsal dinner or any other formalized affair, make sure they receive invitations to these events shortly after they get the wedding invitation so they know they are expected. Otherwise you can plan to have everyone gather on a more impromptu basis for an informal supper, or at hotel poolside for an afternoon of sipping and splashing. Just don't leave your guests to fend entirely for themselves in a strange city.

You and the groom should arrange to be present at least some of the time at any pre-wedding gatherings. Unless it is very late, out-of-towners and others will inevitably end up after the wedding back at your parents' home to continue celebrating and reuniting. If you know that won't be appreciated, try to arrange in advance for another friend or relative to issue a post-reception invitation.

One mother of the bride whose daughter would be residing in a faraway city after the honeymoon found that the continuous stream of visitors for the rest of the wedding weekend was a welcome relief to the loneliness she was already starting to feel. "A house full of people kept me busy laughing and talking, and reminded me that my daughter's new life was a cause for genuine happiness," she admitted.

Remember that your wedding is not a convention, and people should not be expected to check in and report their whereabouts every hour of the day. But one or two social activities you know they will enjoy will make them even more glad they came.

Special Considerations

*B*esides all the myriad details of wedding planning that brides have been managing for decades, changes in society produce still more considerations for today's bride and groom. Our diverse population is a source of national pride, but diversity can also lead to misunderstanding. It is worthwhile, then, to give some forethought to possible problems before they crop up, and to handle conflict gracefully should it occur.

Ethnic Customs

The *coupe de mariage*, an engraved, two-handled cup passed on by French couples for generations; the traditional Irish fruitcake wedding cake—laced with whiskey, of course; the Polish babushka rather than the bridal veil and headpiece; almond "confetti" tossed at an Italian bride and groom—almost every country has its own unique wedding traditions. And many of these traditions have even found their way into general use at American weddings: the tossing of rice (the Orient), the bridal mantilla (Spain), something blue (Israel). After all, our backgrounds contribute to our unique individuality and for many of us, our cultural and religious traditions give special significance to our wedding day.

Whereas once young Americans sought to shed their Old World image, people today seem to be taking a new interest and pride in the traditions of their forefathers. The ethnic wedding is becoming increasingly popular.

Famous bridal gown designer Priscilla of Boston has been quoted as saying that she personally perfers the ethnic wedding to the "boring, uptight society affair," even if it does mean extra work for her to design a gown to withstand the rigors of some ethnic celebrations.[3] As anyone who has ever attended one will tell you, the exuberant joy and communal spirit typical of a traditional Jewish, Polish, Greek, Italian, Mexican, Irish, or any other ethnic wedding is unmatched among social occasions.

Yet strong ethnic traditions, especially conflicting ones, can present problems for brides and grooms who want a different style of wedding from the one their families have in mind. Conflicts may begin with the guest list, concerning the invitations to distant relatives, and may escalate into major family arguments. If your ethnic identity seems to be turning your wedding day into a national holiday, consider some compromises:

Colors and Accents: Many ferns, flowers, herbs, grains, and greens dear to particular nationalities have legendary symbolism. Do a little research to find out what your ethnic group's are, and integrate them into your wedding bouquets or centerpieces. Colors and decorations might also be significant and traditional. A Chinese bride, for instance, could consider using red in her overall color scheme.

Food: Plan your menu to include at least some ethnic dishes compatible with other things you've chosen. A buffet can offer something for everybody—a pasta dish here, smoked fish there, sushi somewhere in between. Those who aren't familiar with the dishes don't have to sample them, but those who expect to find them won't be disappointed.

Customs and Music: Some wedding customs—for example, that of the Bermudians, who plant a little tree, or that of the Indians, who sprinkle flower petals—can be easily adapted to whatever type of ceremony or reception you're having. Again, do some research. As for music, how about an occasional hora or polka during the course of the evening?

The point, as always, is that the wedding is primarily your day, but it also belongs in part to your families. If you decide to go with an all-out ethnic event, wonderful. You deserve a good time. If you decide just to incorporate some ethnic customs into your celebrations, you can be sure that they will bring honor to a very special person—you.

Long Distance/Regional Differences

As one travels America and experiences life in different communities firsthand, one begins to form an impression of the collective personality of each region. Foreign visitors are always struck by the marked differences in speech patterns and social customs, as well as by the obvious physical variations in the land itself.

Such impressions are extremely subjective, of course, based as they are on one's own experience in a given area. But the differences are real nonetheless, and they get even more real when two people from two different regions are trying to plan a wedding.

Tell a New Yorker you're going to have a reception with only cake, punch, and mints in the church hall. Tell a Texan he can't wear boots to a wedding. Ask a southerner from a dry county about facilities for an open bar. Talk to an Iowa farmer about your $20,000 wedding. See how these people look at you. Besides all the hassles of making plans via long distance, there are also some real gaps in understanding to be overcome.

Can such differences be resolved? Of course they can, but it will take communication and patience for each party to understand that his way is not the only way. We all tend to take our own style of life for granted until faced with other ways of living.

As the bride, you will most likely hold the wedding in your community. If the groom is from another area, even fifty miles away, make sure you take the time to explain to him and his family how weddings are usually done in your hometown. Don't assume they know. In return, encourage them to share their expectations for the wedding with you and your family. Try to compromise wherever possible and make them aware of any limitations. Remember, rules of etiquette and social style are relevant only insofar as the local community accepts them.

If you are making any arrangements for your fiancé's parents, like the rehearsal dinner or hotel accommodations for guests, present them with the list of possibilities and let them make the decisions. Be extra careful about informing them of costs and possible alternatives, and allow them the freedom to exercise their own approach without undue pressure from you.

It is especially helpful if your fiancé and his family can come for a pre-wedding visit to meet your own family and friends and to get an idea of how things are done in your area. If members of your wedding party are from far away and not well-known to you, they should also receive extra courtesy and consideration. Whatever you can do to make them more comfortable will be appreciated by all concerned and will minimize opportunities for misunderstanding.

Remarriage

You're being married for the second time. You have informed your family and friends and children (see "Informing the Families," page 15), but you still have some nagging questions: May I have a formal wedding? May I wear white? May my children participate? Is it okay to have a shower? an engagement party? Should

I inform my former spouse? To satisfy your curiosity, the answer to all of these questions is yes, but let's take them one at a time.

A divorced or widowed groom's status has never had any bearing whatsoever on the type of wedding his bride can have. Happily, the same is now true for the bride. Today divorced and widowed women are choosing whatever type of wedding appeals to them. Moreover, many are seizing the opportunity to enjoy the kind of wedding they always wanted but maybe didn't get to have the first time around. All the old taboos centering on a bride's age, virtue, and marital history have pretty much disappeared except in the most conservative communities.

As a bride, you have the right to have any kind of wedding you like and to wear whatever you feel is suitable for the occasion. Moreover, your children from a former marriage can be flower girls or ring bearers, bridesmaids or ushers, or even your best man or maid of honor, as appropriate to their age. And if your father is so inclined, he can walk you down the aisle.

As for pre-wedding parties, enjoy! A marriage is a special occasion, and those who love you will want to share it with you. People who offer to give you parties do so because they care about *you*. Whether you've been widowed or divorced has nothing to do with their affections.

Rarely is a former spouse invited to the wedding, but he or she should probably be told shortly before or after, especially if legal or financial obligations still exist. Here again, though, there may be exceptions to both statements. A widow or widower who is still close to her or his former in-laws may wish to add them to the guest list. Provided the prospective spouse doesn't object (and one really shouldn't), it is certainly appropriate to include them in your newfound happiness.

With remarriages constituting 30 percent of the yearly nuptials in this country, there is no reason for any woman to allow public opinion to dissuade her from having the kind of wedding she wants. However, if you had an extravaganza before, a scaled-down version may be more appropriate this time. If any of your friends or relatives are uncomfortable with what you choose to do, then simply allow them the freedom not to participate. Whatever makes you and those you truly care about happy will be the proper wedding for you.

Canceling

"I just couldn't go through with it," said Nora, twenty-eight, the day after her wedding would have taken place. "It sounds trite, but I really was swept off my feet, and I didn't begin to see what he was like until we got into our plans and closer to the actual wedding. As much as I tried to convince myself otherwise, I just knew it wouldn't work."

Nora broke her engagement and called off her wedding barely one month in advance. Invitations had to be rescinded, engagement and wedding gifts had to be returned, deposits for the reception and some service fees were lost, and her wedding gown, fully fitted and paid for, now hangs in her closet. Nora's decision took a lot of courage.

Looking back, she sees that everything went too fast and that she and her fiancé hardly knew each other at all before they began to plan the wedding. "From day one we disagreed," recalls Nora sadly. "I was able to pass over the disagreements at first, telling myself that they were just silly little arguments over silly little things. But gradually I began to see the same sources of conflict emerge over and over again—money, family, lifestyle. We couldn't even agree on our honeymoon. It got to where I just couldn't dismiss my doubts as pre-wedding jitters."

Will Nora ever plan a big wedding again? Will her parents and friends ever again trust her judgment? Will she overcome the embarrassment and self-doubt this incident has caused her? Though no one can be absolutely sure, Nora's outlook for recovery is good: "The day I did it, the day I told my fiancé and my parents, I felt relieved of a terrible secret. And while I have regretted the hard feelings and some people's reactions, I haven't regretted my decision one minute since."

Had she been less certain of the seriousness of her doubts, Nora might have chosen merely to postpone her wedding rather than to cancel it entirely. Some of the couples we've interviewed have done that and have gone on to have beautiful weddings and happy marriages later. Only the people involved can determine the extent of their misgivings, and only they can resolve them one way or another.

If you find your wedding becoming overshadowed by a persistent cloud of doubt, try to define your fears and analyze the sources of your apprehension. Then discuss them in a calm and honest way with your fiancé. Fears are not logical and don't just go away; anything that bothers you enough to cause you worry is real enough to be discussed.

Should the two of you decide to cancel or postpone your wedding, do so with proper notification to those involved (see "Broken Engagements," page 23) and leave it at that. Lengthy conversations and rueful soul-searching with all your family and friends won't make the decision any easier or any more pleasant to endure. If you feel that those closest to you deserve some explanation for your change in plans, then give it, but keep it rational and devoid of hysteria. The more confident you are about your decision, the more others will respect your right to make it. And you do have that right!

Your Wedding Planning Checklist

Good planning is the key to fulfilling your dreams of the perfect wedding. Use this handy checklist to maintain order in your life during the hectic, happy months ahead.

Your Wedding Planning Checklist

6 TO 12 MONTHS BEFORE THE WEDDING

- Together, visit your clergy. Set the date for the ceremony.
- Discuss expenses with all concerned and establish a firm budget.
- Decide on the size and formality of your wedding.
- Shop for your wedding dress, headpiece, and veil.
- Select two or three possibilities for your attendants' gowns and arrange an appointment with the shop in the next few weeks to bring your attendants in to see the choices. Because they pay for their own dresses, it's thoughtful to do this if possible. The final decision is yours.
- Select the place you'd like to hold the reception. Make reservations if it is in a club, hotel, catering hall, or restaurant. If it is to be at home or at a place that does not provide food, check into catering services and book them. Ask to see a variety of possible menus; inquire if a cake is included or must be arranged separately.
- Draw up the guest list. Notify your fiancé's family to do the same.
- Select your photographer, musicians, and florist. Invite your attendants. Discuss finances with them and try to set an approximate cost for their gowns, headpieces, shoes, and gloves. Be considerate of their limitations.
- Have your fiancé ask his best man and ushers to be in the wedding.
- Discuss honeymoon destination possibilities. Send for brochures.
- Register with the bridal gift registry in your favorite store. Meet with the director of the registry and her trained staff to help you choose your china, silver, crystal, linens, and other household preferences. Think of what you'd like for shower gifts as well as wedding presents.

3 MONTHS BEFORE THE WEDDING

- Select and order your invitations. At the same time, order personal stationery (an ample supply of both letter and note paper) for writing thank-you notes before and after your wedding.
- Plan details of your wedding trip. Traditionally, your fiancé is responsible for making all arrangements—reservations, tickets, etc. But if you're better at that, don't hesitate to offer. Consult a travel agent.

• Have mothers select their dresses. Your mother has the privilege of first choice so that she can have the color and style she prefers. The groom's mother chooses a dress of the same length in a color to complement. Both should blend with your bridal party color scheme.

• Decide upon the men's attire. Accompany your fiancé to a formalwear specialty shop in your locale to select what the groom, best man, ushers, and fathers will wear.

• Begin trousseau shopping. You'll be wearing these clothes during the first year of marriage, so your choices should reflect where and how you are going to live.

• Select your going-away outfit and honeymoon clothes based on your destination.

2 MONTHS BEFORE THE WEDDING

• Plan recording of gifts. From the moment the first gift arrives, keep accurate records either in a special book (there are many designed for this purpose) or on your invitation card files, if that is a better system.

• Keep up with thank-you notes. Try to acknowledge each gift upon arrival to avoid last-minute rush and lengthy delays in extending thanks.

• Finish addressing invitations and announcements. All addressing, stuffing, and stamping should be completed in time to mail the invitations four to six weeks before the wedding.

• Confirm the date and time of the rehearsal with your cleric. Notify attendants and family when and where it will be held.

• Plan a rehearsal dinner. Select time and place, settle upon menu and decorative details with caterer. If out-of-town guests are being included, send invitations to them.

• Arrange accommodations for attendants who do not live in town. If neither you nor family, friends, or neighbors have the facilities to put them up, make hotel reservations. Your fiancé does the same for his attendants. Make reservations for out-of-town guests now as well.

• Select gifts for attendants. Usually the bride gives something personal and permanent to her maids such as a pin or a charm. Remind your fiancé to select presents for his best man and ushers. Some suggestions: tie pin or tack, cuff links, pocket calculator, pen and/or pencil. Engraving, when possible, is a thoughtful gesture.

• Check with local authorities on waiting periods for blood tests necessary for obtaining a marriage license.

• Make an appointment with your doctor for a complete physical examination, blood test, and any advice you may need regarding contraceptive methods.

- Meet with the person handling your reception and firm up all details. If you will need rental equipment, arrange for it now.
- Meet with the musicians who will be playing at the ceremony and those you've engaged for the reception. Go over the list of selections that you and your fiancé want in the program.
- Select the wedding ring(s). Be sure to allow time for engraving.
- Set a date with your photographer to take your formal bridal portrait four weeks before the wedding date.

ONE MONTH BEFORE THE WEDDING

- Have final fitting of your gown and make certain it will be ready to take to your bridal-portrait sitting.
- Make an appointment to have your hair styled just before your formal portrait is taken and again the day before or day of your wedding.
- Check apparel for the wedding party. Have bridemaids' gowns fitted. Get swatches of material and have shoes dyed to match. If any attendants live out of town, send their dresses to them to be fitted. Check mothers' dresses and accessories.
- Call the caterer and make a final decision on the reception menu. Be sure that the cake has been ordered. Give a reliable estimate of the number of guests expected so they can give you a written confirmation of cost per person with an itemized accounting—to the smallest detail—of what they promise to provide.
- Confer with the florist. Be sure the photographer knows what candids you wish to have taken and whether there are particular people—grandparents, aunts, uncles—you want included in your album. Make a list and appoint someone who knows all to guide the photographer.
- Arrange transportation to the ceremony and, if required, from the ceremony to the reception. Plan parking facilities for guests' cars.
- Plan the bridesmaids' luncheon. If you are not having very many attendants and can arrange to entertain them at home, it will lend a more personal touch. Gifts can be presented now or at the rehearsal dinner.
- Select your groom's wedding gift.
- Go over all procedures of the ceremony and receiving line. Make seating plans for the rehearsal dinner (if it is large), for the ceremony, and for the reception. Write out place cards if you plan to have a bride's table and a parents' table. Decide who will be in the receiving line and plan positions.
- Keep gift checklist up to date and *write thank-you notes daily*.
- Consult movers for estimates on moving your gifts and personal belongings to another town, if you will be relocating. Usually these are not moved until

after the wedding, particularly when gifts are to be displayed. Make certain you are insured against damage or loss in transit.

2 WEEKS BEFORE THE WEDDING

• Go with your fiancé to fill out the forms for your marriage certificate.
• Be sure clothing and accessories for all members of the bridal party are in order.
• Settle final details with caterer.
• Check with the society editor of your newspaper and your groom's hometown paper to find out what form they wish you to follow to submit your wedding announcement and photograph. Mail it soon.
• Take care of name changes on your bank account, social security card, license, insurance, etc.
• Attend parties in your honor.

ONE WEEK BEFORE THE WEDDING

• Wrap gifts for your attendant and groom.
• Add guests who have been late in accepting invitations for the reception and give last-minute total count to the caterer.
• Confirm singers, musicians, and recheck selections to be played.
• Remind everyone involved about the rehearsal dinner. Begin arranging your gift display. All cards should be removed. Checks are not displayed but a card stating "Check from Aunt Louise" may be substituted.
• Insure gifts during display.
• Invite friends and relatives to drop by to see your gifts.
• Make a final check with florist, caterer, sexton, cleric, musicians, and photographer.
• Begin honeymoon packing.

ONE DAY BEFORE THE WEDDING

• Attend the rehearsal. Review all duties with the principals in the wedding party.
• Give ushers the list of guests to be seated in the reserved section.

THE WEDDING DAY

• Rest and thoroughly relax in a nice warm bath.
• Allow plenty of time to dress—about two hours before you have to be at the ceremony.
• Have a wonderful day and enjoy every beautiful moment!

Part Three
Your Marriage

Making a Marriage

*H*ow long does the honeymoon last? Answers vary. There are long-married couples who maintain that their honeymoon has never ended and that in fact their relationship has gotten more intense and more exciting with each passing year. Then there are unfortunate couples who admit to a short-lived euphoria, an almost immediate disillusionment with married life from the very beginning. For most people who stay together, the true answer to this question probably rests somewhere in between these extremes.

"All happy families are alike," said the great writer Leo Tolstoy, "but every unhappy one is unhappy in its own way." Harmony in the home appears to come so effortlessly for some; for others, it remains an ever-elusive goal. Couples whose marriages fail can usually tell you why it failed because they have the benefit of hindsight. By contrast, couples who are blessed with good marriages are often unwilling or unable to offer advice to others. While all happy marriages appear alike on the outside, individual partners are keenly aware of the uniqueness of their own relationship. They know that what works for them may not work for others. Thus it is mostly left to psychologists, sociologists, and researchers to attempt to unravel common threads of success.

Authors Ronna Romney and Beppie Harrison went to the experts for their book on the secrets of longevity in marriage. Their experts were numerous so-called ordinary married couples in the kitchens and living rooms of America. Their findings were not startling: "None of the marriages were identical." But their insightful conclusion might be a real news flash for many newly—and not so newly—wed couples: "A good marriage, it seems, is never finished."[1]

In other words, marriage is work—probably the most important, most fulfilling, most unrelenting work of one's life. It means never forgetting, never misplacing, never ignoring the magnitude of the promise you've made. It means living with the toothpaste squeezed in the middle or resorting to separate tubes. It means dropping not-so-subtle hints to a forgetful spouse or learning to put up with forgetfulness. It means pulling pranks and sharing prayers with equal ease. It means enduring the bad times so the good times will be that much sweeter.

Not all marriages can work. Not all marriages should work. But with over half of all divorces occurring within the first seven years of marriage, and an estimated 40 percent within the first four years,[2] one wonders how many simply walk away the first time the going gets rough. Even anthropologist Nena O'Neill, co-author with her late husband of the controversial book *Open Marriage*, recently observed: "We have so many lifestyle options that people don't commit themselves to one long enough to learn to handle a little unhappiness."[3]

No one suggests that every couple who stays together is a happy couple. Nor would anyone in his right mind counsel living in misery for the sake of a long marriage—or even for the sake of the children. But a successful marriage is more than a feat of endurance. Happy couples know that some bad days are inevitable. They're willing to work out difficulties and share disappointments because their overall quality of happiness together far outweighs isolated problems. Their commitment is renewed as each problem is solved, and they are able to go forward with a greater understanding and appreciation of each other. In this way the quality of happiness is enhanced again and again.

After the Wedding

"Being a newlywed is sort of like driving a new car," confessed one bride of three months. "You don't want to be the first one to dent the fender."

The initial weeks and months of married life are a special time, one most couples relish and remember with fondness. They are days of intensity, full of new discoveries and satisfying experiences. These early times together are often funny, sometimes sad, and always an adventure. You are facing the unknown.

No matter how well you think you know yourself and your partner, marriage always brings new revelations. Even couples who have lived together before routinely admit that once they are married, "it's not the same." A new sense of permanence prevails, a legal, public commitment to a future together. Marriage may be just a piece of paper, but from it a new identity emerges.

The two of you are a couple now, partners in life. The psychological shift from "I-me" to "you-we" may be subtle, but it's there. It begins, as well it should, from the very moment your vows are exchanged. Suddenly your life is not your own; it's shared with an ever-present partner. This change can be one of the most challenging adjustments in early married life, and inevitably brings some ambivalent feelings.

There is a tremendous feeling of freedom in the love and security of another person. At the same time, there is also a nostalgia for lost independence. Do you go to the movies without him if he's too tired to go? Is he entitled to continue enjoying his night out with the boys? Should you spend the money for graduate school even though you're both determined to save for a house? You find yourselves driving carefully around each other, afraid of denting that fender.

"Let there be spaces in your togetherness," wrote Kahlil Gibran about marriage,[4] but the size of those spaces can be awfully hard to determine. It requires an understanding—often difficult for the uncertain, eager-to-please newlywed—that togetherness does not necessarily mean physical presence or even like-mindedness. There may well be times in your life together when you will feel that the only thing the two of you share is mutual affection. But that's okay. It happens to the best of friends.

After the excitement of wedding planning and the whirlwind of activities surrounding the wedding, the newlywed often feels some moments of doubt and a bit of an emotional letdown as married life settles into a normal routine. Dr. Anne Tobin-Ashe, family therapist at Georgetown University's Family Center, says that an emotional low following any event of extreme intensity and expectation is inevitable, and she advises newlyweds to plan for it. "Anticipate the celebration of your first month's anniversary," she suggests. "Make plans to share a special activity together, attend a play, shop for furniture, entertain some friends in your new home." In this way you can begin to experience the joys of couplehood and can minimize the normal anxieties about early marital adjustments.

Asserting Your Couplehood

Establishing yourselves as a couple doesn't happen overnight. The recognition of the need for unity arrives swiftly; the methods for meeting that need take years to evolve.

The first fact of couplehood you'll have to wrestle with is each other's idiosyncrasies. We all have them. Nobody is perfect. You'll discover to your horror that the lively, chatty fiancé of the ten o'clock coffee break days at work is a real bear three hours earlier. He'll discover in short order that you're much more comfortable in your flannel bathrobe and fuzzy slippers than in the silk lounging pajamas that you wore on the honeymoon. One of you will fold the towels lengthwise, one of you will fold them crosswise, and the linen closet will be a mess. It's like adjusting to a roommate all over again.

You may be friends and you may be lovers, but you also have to live together. Everyone has their maddening little quirks; the challenge is to keep those little quirks from interfering with more important things. "I never really thought about the disposal of dental floss in our old apartment," admitted Ginny sheepishly. "But suddenly in our new house with our sleek, expensive chrome bathroom accessories, Bob's dental floss drove me crazy!"

Lovers are not mind readers. They take for granted the way they live and the things they do. Some things, like the right to privacy and work habits, deserve to be respected. But other things, small things, can be adjusted easily without hurting anyone's feelings or entailing any great sacrifice. For instance, Ginny and Bob solved the problem of the dental floss by using a plastic liner in the wastebasket. Nevertheless, one partner, in this case Ginny, had to make the other aware of the nuisance and to offer a solution. *Modern Bride*'s 3 Cs—consideration, communication, and compromise—work as well in marriage as they do in wedding planning.

The next realization of what couplehood means will come from outside the home. Chances are that among the things drawing you together in the first place were mutual interests and a shared social circle. Even so, as a couple you will find some friendships and activities from your single life hard to sustain. Your new husband may be very fond of your best friend, Sally, but he still may not want to have her to dinner three times a week.

As time goes on, the interests and preoccupations of your single friends may seem less relevant to your life as a married person. Not that you won't still enjoy or care for your old friends, but changes in one's life situation have a way of altering perceptions and rearranging priorities. (This will happen again and again as you change residences, have children, etc.) One of the nicest things about having friends is that there can be many of them to complement the different facets of our lives. The value of old friends never diminishes, but their place in your life will be shared with new interests and commitments.

By the same token, while your husband will be your best friend, you cannot expect him to fill your every social need or to share your every special interest. That's simply too much to ask. A balance must be struck between the primary importance of your mate and your need for others in your life.

Most newlywed couples find that they begin to develop couple friends, often other newly married couples who share their combined interests and lifestyle. Hence a healthy "yours, mine, and ours" circle of relationships is established. This circle takes the onus of sharing every interest and activity off one's partner. You may have enjoyed an occasional hockey game together when you were engaged, but every game of the season is a bit more than you can handle? Then let him go with a friend.

How much separate activity is too much? Only you can be the judge of that. There are happy couples who have never spent a night away from each other, and there are happy couples who routinely take separate vacations. As a relationship grows, each partner becomes more confident and less possessive of the other. You too will strike that balance between togetherness and independence, but it will take time.

The Marital Partnership

Few modern marriages give one partner complete and absolute dominion over the other. Though it may not always seem so, most decisions in a marriage are made mutually. As is true in any successful business partnership, sound decision making in a marital partnership involves an admission of one's own strengths and weaknesses and a recognition of the other's abilities or areas of expertise. But the division of labor doesn't always work out the way you expect it to.

"My husband has a graduate degree in finance and makes decisions about millions of dollars every day," laughs Samantha, a veteran of fifteen years of marriage. "But meeting the household budget and balancing the checkbook drove him to distraction when we were first married." The result is that Samantha handles all the family finances, including their tax returns, investments, and insurance, and any major decisions on expenditures. "I always tell him what I'm going to do, of course, or caution him when our budget gets a little out of line," she says, "but he never questions my decisions. In spite of his background, I really am better at household management than he is. I can work with two zeros. He can only work with six!"

The allocation of responsibilities and the delineation of spheres of influence require a high level of maturity and self-knowledge. As was discussed in Part I, we are always in danger of slipping into the gender models and sexual stereotypes from our past. Such stereotypes, when they exist, must be discarded for the mutual advantage of both partners. A woman may well choose the traditional role of wife and mother in marriage, but that doesn't mean she has to live her life as the silent partner.

Marital decision making is best achieved through objectivity. Whatever the issue or problem—financial, family, career—if a couple can set emotion aside and look at the merits or shortcomings of a situation purely from the perspective of long-term couplehood, the decision made will be that much more sound and equitable.

Due to Tim's job promotion, Tim, Stacy, and their two children were being relocated from the Midwest to a large northeastern city. The family was excited about the move, and all of them were happy about Tim's chance to advance. However, when Stacy had to choose between an urban residence close to Tim's office and a more spacious home over an hour away in the suburbs, she was tempted to veto the move altogether. She knew the sacrifice a long daily commute would entail for Tim, but she had also spent most of her life in the suburbs and was fearful of adapting to an urban environment.

Stacy could have jeopardized Tim's career by refusing to move, or she could have been selfish and forced an additional strain on Tim for the sake of her own security and convenience. Instead she chose to learn more about the amenities of city life and to place top priority on Tim's time with the family. In the end she chose the urban location and everyone, including the children, benefited from meeting the new challenges of city life.

Often our own fears and prejudices keep us from thinking straight. If we can get past our own egos, we can eliminate the divisiveness that endangers couplehood.

Outside the Home

There are other threats to couplehood, other situations calling for a unified we. For most couples, the first major test of their couplehood arises in dealing with their families. Not only do you bring the baggage of your own parents, grandparents, sisters, brothers, aunts, uncles, nieces, nephews, and cousins to your marriage, but you also find another set of luggage in place when you arrive! Almost immediately, as if by decree, you find yourselves having inane conversations about your families, even arguing about them.

"What should I call your mother? She's not *my* mom."

"I don't think your dad likes me very much."

"Your sister's okay, but that husband of hers is a jerk."

"I wish your parents would call first."

"But I promised my mother we'd be *there* on Christmas Eve."

And so it goes, on into an eternity of trivial disputes—whose house? whose turn? who says? Even the best of families can be a mixed blessing, if for no other reason than that they kill you with kindness.

Let's face it. You're the newcomer and you will be put to the test. You will have to prove that you truly love your spouse and that you are the best wife or husband anyone could hope for. If you have religious or cultural or racial or socioeconomic differences, you will simply have to change the family's definition of best. It's not impossible, it can be done.

Mostly, integrating one's self into another's family and both families into the life of the couple is accomplished through trial and error with time and patience. Above all, never let the families pull you apart. You two may disagree on issues privately at home, but you must never give either family any cause for choosing sides. Families don't break up marriages; couples do it to themselves.

"You're your mother's son, all right," jokes Nancy as her husband, Paul, scurries by with paint, roller, and ladder in hand.

"I know," he quips. "We have special activity genes."

There was a time, Nancy confides, when she wouldn't have joked about Paul's endless projects and whirlwind activities around the house. She explains why:

"When Paul and I were first married and his mother would come to visit, the two of them would leave me breathless. We could never just sit and talk. We always had to be *doing* something. I felt guilty because I didn't have their energy, and resentful because I never seemed to be a part of things."

Several years of marriage and more than a few discussions later, Nancy and Paul—and her mother-in-law—now understand one another and respect one another's style of getting things done. "Paul and his mother are both highly energetic people, while I prefer to do things more slowly, plan more carefully. It took me a long time to realize that neither of them ever meant to imply I was lazy."

Not only has Nancy come to appreciate Paul's industriousness, she's even grateful for all the extra chores that get done when the "white tornado" visits. "I keep threatening to hire them out," laughs Nancy. "They can do all the work while I sit quietly counting all the money."

Ironically, even the most meddlesome mother-in-law wants you to make it, wants you to define your terms and stake out your territory just as she did years ago. Most in-laws want to know you, to respect you, and to love you. And though you may have difficulty believing it at times, their actions are motivated toward that end. But they, like your spouse, are not omniscient. They cannot always know how you feel or where you stand unless you tell them.

If you're not accustomed to drop-in company, say so. If certain subjects are off limits conversationally, let that be known. If there is a conflict between families on holidays, discuss the problem openly. Above all, don't allow yourselves to fall into a pattern of behavior and expectations you have no intention of maintaining. Remember that a precedent, once set, is harder to break.

In order to become a couple you must have privacy, perhaps at the beginning more than at any other time. You must seek to minimize the intrusion of family opinions and politics into your own lives. You must strive for independence, financial and emotional, in order to be recognized as a viable family unit of your own. It is hard enough for two people to make decisions about their lives. When those decisions are put on the agenda of a family council, a consensus will never be reached.

Later in your married life, after you have become loved and accepted for the person you are rather than for the person you married, you will have time to develop real and lasting relationships with your in-laws as people, one to one. For now, though, be content to be part of a couple—a strong one.

Finally, a word about loyalty. Loyalty is just another word for the commitment you've made to your decision and to the person you love. Loyalty means standing by your mate when he/she has made a mistake. It means taking up for the other when he/she is wrongfully accused or misunderstood. It means being prepared to fight along with your spouse, or to do the fighting for him when he can't do it for himself.

People don't speak much of loyalty anymore, nor do they notice the many examples of heroism in daily life. But the examples are all around us if we look. The wife who holds her head high even though her husband has been convicted of a crime. The husband who sits patiently at his wife's bedside in the hospital. The couple who cling to each other in grief. These are not starry-eyed idealists who can't accept reality or who suffer from false pride. No, these are people who know the facts and can be loyal to each other in spite of them. They are people just like you: people who have discovered what love really means.

Love and the Laundry

Perhaps two people can live as cheaply as one, but they certainly can't live as easily. First of all, there's twice as much laundry, and not always another pair of hands to help wash and iron it.

The phone rang in the middle of the afternoon and Erica skipped in from the backyard to pick it up.

"Hello," said the lady's voice on the other end. "May I speak to your mother?"

"She's away on a business trip right now," answered Erica. "Can my dad help you?"

"Well, this is Mrs. March from church. I was calling to ask your mother if she could make a casserole for our youth group supper, but I'll just call back another time."

"That won't do you any good," interjected Erica matter-of-factly. "My mom doesn't cook. She does the laundry. I think you want to speak to my dad."

More and more the division of labor in a household is less influenced by roles or even talents than it is by time. You do what has to be done because you're there and because you have a few minutes available in which to do it. In the case of Erica's parents, her mom travels a lot and commutes thirty-five miles to her job. Erica's dad, on the other hand, works nearby and has always had a more flexible work schedule. In their household, Dad cooks and supervises children, Mom does the laundry—some evenings and on weekends. Everybody cleans as they go along.

This busy family is not at all atypical of the average American family today. People in such households soon shed the shackles of sex-role stereotyping in the interest of time and efficiency. They are flexible yet secure. They know that their love for each other does not depend on who does the dishes or the laundry.

Family lifestyles develop and change over time. As the situation changes, through promotions at work or the addition of children, so do the mechanics of running a household. So do priorities.

In the first half of this century, most women did not work outside the home and were therefore almost fully responsible for housekeeping and child-rearing. For a variety of reasons, not the least of which were economic, that situation has changed dramatically since World War II, and it will continue to do so.

John Naisbitt, a social forecaster who is chairman of a Washington-based research firm and author of the best-selling *Megatrends*, predicts that by 1990 only 14 percent of husband and wife households will consist of one working spouse, and wives will contribute 40 percent of the total family income.[5] By the year 2000, 85 percent of all women will be in the work force.[6] With projections like that, American families will be even busier in the future than they are now!

Whether men work and women stay home, women work and men stay home, or both work and nobody stays home, the amount of energy and work running a house entails is staggering. Let's just take a look at some of the routine chores: cooking, cleaning, dishwashing, shopping, errands, banking, record keeping, bill-paying, household repairs, yardwork, and of course laundry. Obviously this list is incomplete. You have to add any outside demands from your job or career, time for personal health care and grooming, and some social life, if you have any time or money left over for one. Oh, and never mind about the children. That's a different list.

If just reading this makes you tired, think how you'll feel after living it. Yet there is a bright side. Many of these chores would have to be done anyway even if you were living alone, and almost all of them are more fun, or at least more bearable, when they're done together.

The division of labor in your household is up to the two of you. Some couples trade off tasks: some pick the ones they do best or mind least and stick with them. Nowhere is it written in stone that a woman can't mow a lawn or a man can't dust the furniture. You just have to come to some arrangement whereby everything gets done and no one feels unduly burdened.

"People tease me all the time, even chide me, when I stop what I'm doing to get Jules a cup of coffee," confides Harriet, a professional woman with strong feminist leanings. "But the truth is, if it's snowing outside and I ask him to get dressed and run out and pick up some milk and cigarettes for me, he'll do it without a murmur. A little pampering on both sides makes for a twenty-five-year marriage."

Financial Partnership

In three out of four of the types of couples we studied, we find that
the amount of money a person earns—in comparison with a partner's

income—establishes relative power. This seems a rather cynical finding, one that does not accord well with cherished American beliefs about fairness and how people acquire influence in romantic relationships. Most people like to think that the right to effect decisions is based on the demands of daily events, on which partner is wiser on a certain issue, or on special gifts of persuasion. They do not like to think that income, something that comes into the relationship from the outside, imposes a hierarchy on the couple. But it does.[7]

In their nationwide eighteen-year study of American couples, Drs. Philip Blumstein and Pepper Schwartz of the University of Washington have become the first social researchers to deal in any real depth with the issue of money and relationships. Researchers, like everyone else, are disinclined to deal with the subject of money. Blumstein's and Schwartz's finding may explain why.

We've all heard the old maxim "friendship and money don't mix." Yet in marriage two friends must of necessity mix their money matters. When even the IRS routinely penalizes us for being married, no wonder money becomes a major point of marital contention.[8]

As newlyweds you must deal with finances openly and honestly. Unfortunately, money is such a standard measure of worth and success in our society that it becomes a difficult subject to approach impartially. We come to the discussion with predetermined ideas of status, power, or security, and find our own personal hang-ups and habits with money hard to leave behind.

All of this notwithstanding, discuss it you must. In order to remain fiscally solvent as a couple, you will have to agree on a basic financial philosophy, overall methods of management, and the particular details of cash flow. The resolution of these issues will make your GMP (Good Money Partnership).

Your GMP (Good Money Partnership)

Here are some questions to consider and discuss as you work out your GMP.

- What is your present income?
- What are your fixed monthly expenses?
- What financial resources, if any, have you brought to the marriage?
- What is your income potential in five years? ten years? twenty years?
- Do you have any outstanding or impending major financial obligations—school loans, child support, mortgage, etc.?
- Outside of present necessities, do you have a priority list for future purchases?
- Is it your dream to be a homeowner? If so, how will you achieve it?
- What is your lifestyle? Do you have expensive hobbies and interests, extensive entertainment costs, or a fondness for material goods?
- Are you financially prepared for the unexpected—illness, fire, accidents?
- How important is long-term financial security—life insurance, retirement programs, savings plans?
- Have you ever taken a financial risk—stocks, bonds, other investments?
- Are you strictly of the cash and carry school, or do you believe in credit? If so, what kind and to what degree?
- Would you tend to save for a large purchase, like bedroom furniture, or would you buy it now on an installment plan?
- Will you have credit cards? How will you use them, and who will be responsible for them?
- Will you have a joint checking/savings account, separate accounts, or both?
- If both of you are working, how will you allocate your combined salaries?
- If one of you is not working, what kind of financial independence will he or she enjoy?
- How will extra money be spent, and at whose discretion?
- Will each individual have money strictly for his/her own personal use, or will all funds and spending decisions be jointly shared?
- Who will be responsible for monitoring the budget?
- Who will maintain all records: tax receipts, warranties and service agreements, automobile and homeownership records, insurance policies and loan contracts?
- How will you pay bills—monthly, biweekly, or as they come in? Who will be responsible for the paperwork?
- Who will oversee long-term items—investments, insurance, property taxes, etc.?
- Will yearly taxes be compiled by one of you or both of you, or by a professional?

With all the money management services and investment options available today, couples who plan wisely and spend prudently can build a firm financial foundation for their marriage. If you find that you are not as knowledgeable about money matters as you should be, educate yourself. Many excellent books and magazines on the market deal with every facet of financial planning.[9] It pays to have words like *CD*, *Keogh Plan*, *IRA*, *NOW Account*, *money market*, and *tax-deferred* in your vocabulary.

Above all, find a reputable banker, insurance agent, tax accountant, stock broker, or any other financial advisor you may need. You should never make any major monetary investments or decisions without the guidance of an experienced professional.

The Household Budget

Once you have determined your financial priorities and have agreed on methods of management, you'll want to compile a working household budget. (See the sample budget on page 178.) This budget may have to be adjusted from time to time to reflect changes in income and expenses, and it will probably take a few months for the two of you to do as well in real life as you do on paper. While some couples will have to be more rigid than others, all should have a budget and should try to allow for some flexibility in their plan.

Before you draw up your monthly budget, you will have to estimate your overall yearly income and expenses. Some items, like taxes, insurance premiums, or vacations, occur at certain times of the year only, but must be allocated on a monthly basis. Other items, like food, clothing, and utilities, will require a few months of record keeping before you can determine a monthly average. You may, however, estimate these expenditures by going over your canceled checks, credit card statements, and other receipts. This will give you a good idea of your overall yearly financial picture. From that point you can go on to devise a more detailed monthly budget.

Before we leave the subject of money, here are some facts you should know. First, whether you are an ardent believer in credit or not, you must establish a credit rating, and that can only be done through using and paying back department store charge accounts, credit cards, and small loans. If you ever intend to finance a major purchase like a car or a home, then you will need a good credit history to do so.

Married women have the right, under the law, to establish and maintain credit accounts in their own names. All businesses that offer charge accounts must keep the account records in the names of both spouses *if requested to do so*. Make sure you request it. This way even wives who stay at home can have a personal credit history that is not affected by the death or divorce of a spouse.

Budgeting for Two

WEEKLY INCOME

$_____ His
$_____ Hers
$_____ (Other)
$_____ Total

FIXED LIVING EXPENSES (Monthly)

$_____ Rent/mortgage
$_____ Electric
$_____ Telephone
$_____ Water
$_____ Gas
$_____ Total

Total × 12 = $_____
$_____ ÷ 52 = Weekly Total

ANNUAL FIXED PERIODIC PAYMENTS

$_____ Insurance
$_____ Loans
$_____ Medical
$_____ (Other)
$_____ Total

Total ÷ 52 = $_____ Weekly Total

TOTAL FIXED EXPENSES

$_____

PROJECTED WEEKLY SAVINGS

$_____ Total

FLEXIBLE LIVING EXPENSES (Weekly)

$_____ Groceries
$_____ Transportation
$_____ Laundry/dry cleaners
$_____ Entertainment
$_____ Gifts/contributions
$_____ His personal expenses
$_____ Her personal expenses
$_____ Household maintenance
$_____ (Other)
$_____ Weekly Total

ANNUAL FLEXIBLE EXPENSES

$_____ Her clothing
$_____ His clothing
$_____ Travel
$_____ (Other)
$_____ Total

Total ÷ 52 =
$_____ Weekly Total

TOTAL FLEXIBLE EXPENSES

$_____

Total Income − Total Fixed Expenses =
Total Amount Available* for Flexible Expenses

If total available for flexible expenses exceeds your projection, adjust your spending habits (entertaining, clothing). If the total is under, consider increasing weekly savings for emergencies and inflation.

Second, the Equal Credit Opportunity Act of 1974 forbids credit discrimination on the basis of sex or marital status. Accordingly, when you apply as a couple for a loan or mortgage, the income of both spouses must be considered. No one can ask you if you intend to keep on working.

Last, names make a difference, and so do little words like *and* and *or*. A husband and wife are not legally one entity in terms of the ownership of property, money, or securities. In the interest of harmony and balance, you should each maintain separate ownership of some things. You should thoroughly investigate the pros and cons before transferring ownership to the other or putting things into joint ownership. A home acquired together, for instance, might be held in both names, while a rental property you owned before marriage might stay in your own name. Ownership and property laws vary from state to state, so get good legal advice before making any major decisions.

Likewise, bank accounts can be held jointly or separately. A joint savings account held by Mary Doe *and* John Doe means that both permissions are needed for transfer of funds. An account held as Mary Doe *or* John Doe allows each partner independent transactional privileges. A major advantage of the latter type is that it allows immediate access in the event of the disability or death of your partner. Even with your own separate checking account, you may want your partner to have signatory powers so that funds would not become frozen in the event of your disability or death.

All of these points are worth thinking about and discussing. Remember: in the event of the unexpected, what you don't know *can* hurt you.[10]

Dual-Career Couples

The subject of money inevitably leads to the topic of work, so this is as good a time as any to discuss the particular problems of the working couple. The issues here go beyond the obvious ones of roles, money, or power. They go to the very heart of your relationship. With the number of dual-income married households (62 percent of all married households) on the rise, the role of work in the lives of both partners in a marriage is too important not to be carefully examined.

Dr. Ida Davidoff, family therapist and visiting lecturer at the Albert Einstein College of Medicine, gives us a perspective on the issue. "It is a fallacy to think that the dual-career household is a new phenomenon, because women have always been the work partners of their men. In the agrarian society, they worked in the fields. In the industrial era, they worked alongside their men in the factories. The difference now is that women in large numbers are working *outside* the family and competing in the same work areas and at the same work levels as men."

What this means is a real challenge to the way we live as couples. No longer is it only the male who is justifiably tired and inattentive after a hard day. No longer is it only the male who suffers the anxieties of job pressure. No longer is it only the male who deserves to be excused from household duties because he has done a full day's work elsewhere.

Beyond the questions of chores and money, the emotional and psychological needs of each spouse must be met. Who is going to listen to whom? Who is going to console? Who is going to understand and support? The relationship itself demands time and attention, and the woman cannot be the sole emotional caretaker. For inexpressive males who have been brought up by society to take support rather than to give it, sharing this role is a challenging dimension of married life.

If you are a dual-career couple, you must remain flexible in your attitudes and recognize the additional stress on your relationship that outside forces create. What will you have to do to compensate for those outside pressures? It's one thing to work late every night when you're single, for instance, but how many nights a week can you expect your spouse to cheerfully have dinner alone? Each partner will have to learn to listen more closely, to recognize that he or she is not always right and that his or her solution to a problem is not always the best or only solution. Some couples will hire household help. Some will get away regularly to private weekend retreats. Some will eat out every night. Others will cut corners and find options in less expensive ways, but all will juggle priorities. Maybe the house will be a little dirtier to leave time for fun on the weekend, or some extra socks and underwear will allow the laundry to go longer between washings. Whatever the problems or solutions, respect for the partner, for his/her emotional, psychological, and physical well-being, must always come first.

Obviously, the ease of reconciling the needs of work and home depends on the extent of the demands made outside the home. There is a very real distinction, for instance, between just working and long-term dedication to a career. The young wife who is working to earn money for the purchase of a house but who does not plan to work forever will not be as preoccupied or pressured as the female MBA seeking to climb the corporate ladder to success. The difference is one of attitude about the job. The woman who works only for financial reasons may be no less tired when she gets home and no less emotionally spent, but—in sharp contrast to the female MBA—she has not put her reputation and self-identity on the line every day at the office.

The image of the male as provider has always led to the definition of a man in terms of his occupation. Now the same thing is happening to a whole new generation of career-minded women. Women no longer have to marry up to achieve status and community recognition; they can achieve those things for themselves. Moreover, current statistics indicate that 12 percent of all working wives now earn more than their husbands, and that figure promises to grow as equal pay for equal work becomes a reality.

The truly dual-career couple, then, has even deeper psychological and emotional issues to settle between them, issues going to the very source of their self-worth.

Indifference is the real killer here, indifference to the needs of the relationship in light of personal career aspirations. And this is increasingly no less true for women than for men. For example, what will happen if one of you is transferred? How will you handle the interruption of your career(s) when starting a family? Will you as a couple be greater than the sum of your parts, or will individual competition override your combined strengths? Career versus family may be an old debate, but it is not trite when you're living it.

People grow and change and their lives move in different directions. What is of paramount importance today may not even matter at all in the days and years to come. Career-working couples don't necessarily have more problems than anyone else, they just have different ones. They are constantly juggling "your goals, my goals, and our goals." As millions of successful working couples demonstrate every day everywhere, a balance can be struck—as long as "our goals" are more important than the other two.

Traditional Couples

Marital adjustments are also necessary for couples in which the husband works and the wife tends the home. These couples, too, will have to determine their roles within the new partnership, roles no longer as clearly defined and universally accepted as they once were.

After a generation of disregard, the role of homemaker is once again becoming valued. As lawmakers study the feasibility of recognizing the homemaker under social security, and as various estimates place the dollar value of full-time homemaker services at around $40,000 a year, there is an increased recognition of the valuable family contribution made by the so-called nonworking spouse.

Staying at home is not for everybody. But for the woman—or man—who does not need the additional income from outside employment and who truly prefers domestic pursuits, it is a valid lifestyle choice. Staying at home does not mean one is a bubblehead, nor does it mean that one's activities are confined to cooking and cleaning. The nation's major political, cultural, and philanthropic organizations would be the first to applaud the accomplishments of intelligent, concerned volunteers who have historically been "just housewives."

Contrary to popular notions, the truly professional homemaker does not spend her days watching soap operas and coffee klatching. Besides the ever-present cooking, cleaning, laundry, and shopping—enough to keep anybody busy—she may also sew, bake, garden, refinish furniture, or hang wallpaper. She probably handles the banking and the bills, runs all the routine errands, and takes care of all the correspondence. In her "free" time, she may enjoy a hobby or two or devote her efforts to church, school, or community activities. If she has children, caring for them will barely leave time for her other responsibilities.

Today's full-time homemaker may derive pleasure from household pursuits, but she will not happily assume the role of resident maid. She is aware of the value of her time and talents, and rightfully expects to be a full and equal partner in the marriage relationship. She knows that without the freedom her home management offers, her husband would find it difficult, if not impossible, to devote his energies to career goals and to enjoy the quality of family life that they share. The successful traditional marriage is built on mutual respect and appreciation for the contribution of each partner, just like the dual-career marriage.

At first this understanding may be more difficult for the traditional couple to achieve. A young woman, particularly one who worked before marriage, might feel guilty about not earning an income and might be reluctant to claim an equal say in her partnership. A young man may not want his wife to work because of an outdated sense of male pride rather than a real appreciation of her domestic talents. There are even women who feel compelled to have children right away as a rationale for not working outside the home. Such attitudes will have to be confronted openly and honestly before a real understanding of marital roles can be reached.

As a full-time wife and/or mother, your home and family *are* your career. But to some extent your husband's career is also yours. Because his income is your source of support, it is wise to be sensitive to the demands of his work and knowledgeable enough to help him any way you can. What's wrong with entertaining corporate clients or offering to pitch in with weekend paperwork when you both have a vested interest in his success?

The choice to stay at home should be one freely made, one from which you can derive a real sense of pride and accomplishment. If you find that you are lonely or bored, resentful of your husband's career or defensive about what you do all day, then you may need to reevaluate your decision.

Recognize, too, that choosing a career at home is almost a luxury in today's world, and that you might not always be able to afford that luxury. Whether or not you ever combine your homemaking activities with marketable interests and experiences, you should always participate fully in family decision making and money management. A woman may be able to afford not to work, but she can never afford to be ignorant about her own affairs or the realities of the world around her.

Sexual Adjustments

Most of us are taught life's basics. We can cook, clean, read, write, drive, sew, and generally take care of ourselves. Yet precious few of us are ever taught how to be lovers. Oh, we may get a course or two in reproduction and we may even be lucky enough to grow up in a warm, affectionate family, but we still know surprisingly little about our own sexuality. Thus satisfying sexual relationships tend to become a matter of trial and error, and unfortunately, poor sexual experiences all too often evolve into a regular pattern of unfulfilling behavior.

In rebellion against the sexual austerity of our Puritan forefathers, we underwent a sexual revolution in the early 1970s. But rather than resulting in true sexual liberation and education, it seems to have led simply to the proliferation of misinformation and the promotion of promiscuity. Many people are still as ignorant and dissatisfied about their sex lives as they ever were. Furthermore, the increased publicity about multiple orgasms, frequency of intercourse, and the like has created artificial standards of sexual adequacy, needlessly making some people feel inadequate in comparison.

First, let's get one fact straight. Whether you experienced sex before marriage or not, lived with your partner before marriage or not, were married before to someone else or not, satisfying sex with your present spouse is a learned behavior. It takes time, practice, patience, and above all, communication. No two people are just made for each other. They may be compatible in terms of sexual appetite, but they are going to have to perfect their sexual technique. To do this, partners must be willing to learn about the intricacies of each other's body and what pleases each the most.

Sexual fulfillment is on ongoing process that doesn't just happen overnight. Moreover, as two people become more familiar with each other, their ways of relating, of being stimulated, may have to change. Other factors also influence sex lives. Job pressures, financial worries, physical fatigue, medication, family conditioning—all adversely affect sexual performance and desire.

Although there are couples who report that the *only* good thing about their marriage is their sex life, those couples are rare. It is estimated that inadequate sexual adjustment plays a significant role in over half of all divorces, and that chronic sexual problems generally have their beginnings within the first two years of marriage. So don't be disappointed if the earth doesn't move and bells don't ring on your first night together. But *do* be prepared to work at achieving sexual fulfillment. Your marriage will benefit immeasurably, and this kind of work is fun!

To begin with, you should know that there are four very common sexual problems which can happen to couples of any age. All can be overcome with the assistance of a qualified sex therapist.

1. Failure to experience orgasm—most commonly in the female, but can also be true of the male. Caused by inexperience, lack of knowledge, or unwillingness to communicate.
2. Premature ejaculation—the male's coming to a climax too rapidly, before the female partner is fulfilled. A learned pattern in the male originating from inexperience or the wrong kind of experience and allowed to continue.

3.   Vaginismus—a tightening of the female vaginal muscles which makes intercourse impossible.

4.   Dyspareunia—a female fear of the pain of penetration. Could have a physiological cause (vaginal infection or scars), but more often does not.

If you are experiencing any of these difficulties, by all means get professional help. Your local teaching hospital or medical center can usually refer you to a therapist in your area. Although you may feel embarrassed at first about bringing a stranger into the privacy of your sex life, it's well worth it. In the hands of a qualified sex therapist, you will quickly feel at ease, and you can save yourself many years of unhappiness and frustration.

In addition, certain illnesses, drugs, and medications can produce sexual side effects. Check with your doctor if you think this could apply to you.

Remember that mutual satisfaction is the key ingredient for a fulfilling sex life. One's own pleasure is a source of pleasure for one's partner. Thus it is up to you to talk about sex, to learn about it, to experiment with each other, and to let your partner know what pleases you. Without this openness, an atmosphere of resentment and frustration develops, and blame and guilt soon come to replace intimacy.

Stella Mostel, M.S., a certified sexual therapist, a lecturer at the New York University School of Medicine, and codirector of the Stamford Center of Human Sexuality, offers this advice for newlywed couples seeking to establish a rewarding sexual relationship: "Forget all you think you know, or didn't know, about sex from the past and concentrate on the here and now, this relationship. Educate yourselves. Express your needs, wants, and desires to each other. You don't, however, want to talk about former sexual partners, nor should you discuss your most intimate personal fantasies—your mate may not share them. If you feel you have a sexual adjustment problem, seek help. Most such difficulties are easily corrected. It could save you years of needless anxiety, and it could even save your marriage."

Sexuality is a complex part of our being, a valuable way of relating to others. Likewise, the act of lovemaking is a most intimate form of communication. Through it, we can bring support, pleasure, and happiness into other areas of our lives. And let's not forget that sex is also good exercise and an eternally popular form of adult recreation!

Retaining Romance

One of the greatest fallacies about romance comes from the notion that in order for an event to be romantic, it must be spontaneous. Actually, nothing is farther from the truth. How often during courtship did you plan ahead what you were going to wear or do or say on a certain evening? How far in advance did you shop for a particular gift or draw up the menu for a special meal? The best, most emotionally satisfying moments in our lives may seem as if they happen spontaneously, but in reality they rarely happen without forethought and anticipation.

The complacency that comes with familiarity in married life is a constant threat. As the years go by, as the first flush of excitement fades and we settle into the routines of daily living, it becomes increasingly difficult not to take the love and presence of one's mate for granted. We start by dropping the most common courtesies, the pleases and thank-yous anyone has a right to expect. Then we begin to assume that mere physical presence means care and attention. Finally we eliminate planned spontaneity from our list of priorities.

"I am constantly amazed," reflects one marriage counselor, "at how many couples do and say things to each other—or neglect to do and say things—that they wouldn't dream of doing or saying to their worst enemies." She smiles sadly. "Then they come in here and wonder what's gone wrong with their marriage."

Romance. It's a simple word that we cloud in mystery, but it really isn't mysterious at all. It is mainly just common sense, consciousness of another human being and respect for his or her needs and feelings. The very preparation and forethought that romance entails in marriage is the greatest, most romantic compliment you can give.

Here are some ways you can keep romance alive in your relationship. Remember, though, it's more fun to think them up yourselves—together.

- Don't let common courtesies slip away along with compliments on your spouse's appearance, talents, etc.
- Dress for each other when possible. Choose a party outfit in his favorite color or an after-shave she especially likes.
- Surprise each other with small things: silly cards, a single flower, the doing of some household chore.
- Recognize the importance of the gentle touch, the subtle flirtation, and the private signals of love between you.
- Plan a special dinner, trip, or outing you know your spouse would enjoy.
- Communicate about your love. Say "I love you," and talk about the reasons why.
- Reserve time for the two of you to be together and enhance that time with music, wine, candlelight, whatever creates a mood for you.
- Make an occasion out of the ordinary. Besides Valentine's Day, there is also the Fourth of July, your fourteenth-month anniversary, or even your very own Let's Hear It for Marriage Day!

The concern here is not how you keep romance alive in your marriage, but that you resolve to work at it. And by the way, there's always room for a good old-fashioned box of candy—even if it does have to be dietetic.

Creative Conflict

Newlywed couples are never prepared for the realities of married life. How could they be? They've never lived it before—at least not with this partner. No matter how many stormy relationships we have previously endured, we always somehow believe that this partner, this union, will be different. This time everything will be perfect.

Part of this fantasy arises out of our idealized notions of true love, which we've already discussed (see Part I). Part of it comes admittedly from books like this one, with beautiful people on the cover and a whole host of problem-solving techniques inside. We are at once frightened by the realities around us and convinced that love and patience can conquer all.

Your spouse is the most important, most powerful person in your world. He is your best friend, your lover, your roommate, your business partner, your counselor, and perhaps the father of your children. He has the ability to make your days sunny, your nights exciting, and your life a legend of love. With so much promise invested in one person, doesn't it also follow that he has the greatest ability to inflict pain? Love and hate flow from the same emotional well, you know.

Perhaps the greatest single discovery that newly married people have to make about each other is that while they are a loving, unified couple, they are also two separate individuals. Being part of a couple does not mean being extensions of each other. In striking a balance between oneness and separateness, conflict is inevitable.

Sociologists tell us that, because little girls are conditioned to be more attuned to social interaction, they grow up expecting more from their relationships. They are taught to be nice and accommodating, to take time and seek depth, to express emotion and value warmth. Men, on the other hand, are raised to get on with it, to get the job done. Whether in sports, in business, or in war, they have been conditioned to deal with competition, conflict, and hostility.

Thus it is not surprising that women routinely express more dissatisfaction and disillusionment in marriage than men do. And much of their disappointment comes from their own inability to handle anger and conflict in a constructive way.

Most of our anger in marriage comes from fear. "You must not love me if you . . ." "How can you say that to me?" "What do you want from me?" The realization of our emotional and sometimes physical or financial dependency on this other person frightens us. So, arguments over the mundane issues of daily life seem to threaten the very love that binds us together.

Put two people in a room and you set the stage for conflict. Add more people and you increase the chances of conflict. Why should marriage and the family be any different? People who respect each other disagree. People who disagree with each other argue. People who love each other work out their differences or agree to disagree and go on to differ again.

There are two possible ways of handling conflict in marriage: to confront or to retreat. Equal partners who respect each other and believe in trust and communication will choose the first. Unequal partners who are unsure of themselves or their loved one will chicken out. When one asks, "What's wrong?" the other will respond, "Nothing," establishing a routine of suppressed anger and guilt. Silence is manipulative, and while it may keep the peace for a while, it breeds a lot of resentment over the long haul.

Everyone has different ways of showing anger. Some will throw things or slam doors, others will sulk or walk away. In marriage, you must learn to recognize both your own patterns of behavior and those of your partner. Learn to accept your partner's style, even if it's different from your own—unless it's truly destructive. For example, if you scream in an argument and your spouse sulks, that's okay as long as you eventually get around to discussing the issues constructively. But if you hurl insults or he refuses to talk at all, that's not okay because you are punishing each other instead of simply expressing anger and then moving on to solve the problem.

A famous movie star recently admitted on television that she buys cheap dishes in the discount store so she will have something to smash when she's mad. She added that she and her husband then always have a good laugh about her throwing techniques while they clean up the mess. While many might be unnerved at the thought of regular china-crashing episodes, the movie star's outlet is essentially harmless and her fury blows over quickly. Since her husband accepts her smashing as a humorous quirk, they are able to get beyond the first explosion of anger to work out the underlying problem.

Sometimes anger gets misdirected. It has come from other sources and has little or nothing to do with one's mate. If your husband snaps at you about the sorry state of the living room because the pressure at work is getting to him, a discussion of housecleaning will not help. With time you will learn to see behind the words and to understand what is really bothering you or your partner.

Real love means affection in spite of differences, and sometimes because of them. To express displeasure with your partner's actions or hurt at your partner's words does not mean that love has gone. In fact it opens the way for a new awareness and understanding of our differences, which paradoxically can strengthen the love relationship. Issues get settled, compromises get made, and respect for individuality continues to grow. Time and energy are not wasted on past disappointments but are directed toward future fulfillment.

Again, how much conflict is too much conflict? One of the wisest answers to that dilemma comes from a highly respected, much-loved teacher on the occasion of her retirement after forty years with especially difficult students. When asked what made her so successful, she replied, "The secret of dealing with people is knowing when to make an issue of something, and when to pretend you didn't notice it."

Second Marriage

One in three marriages involves a spouse who has been married before. Even though the partners may be a bit older, their first years together are not unlike those of other newlyweds. They will still enjoy the excitement and pleasures of the new life they share. They will still have family, financial, and career priorities to sort, and personal needs and habits to adjust.

In other ways, however, second marriages often involve issues more common to couples who have been married several years. Six out of ten second marriages begin with children from a former marriage. And while children may be a joy, they will certainly place demands on the new couple's life together.

Children from a former marriage create an instant extended family for the newlyweds. If you or your partner has full custody of the children, then they will be part of your lives on a daily basis, as they are in any family. Meeting their mental, physical, and emotional needs will demand time and attention from both of you. If the children are not in residence, you will still have to adjust your routine to accommodate their visits, their special occasions, and perhaps even their emergencies.

Along with children come a whole range of other family and financial issues: acceptance of a stepparent, relationship with a former spouse, relationships with grandparents and other relatives, child support and/or alimony. These issues, if not resolved early on, can be further complicated if and when the two of you decide to have children of your own.

The most difficult part of remarriage with children is probably learning to be a stepparent. In most cases, the children will challenge the new stepparent in every way possible. To them the newcomer represents an intrusion and an obstacle to their own parents' getting back together. If one of the parents is dead, the children will feel you are a poor substitute and may even resent their remaining parent's willingness to replace the parent they are still mourning.

As a stepparent, you will have to be firm, patient, and understanding during the difficult adjustment period—even though you are occupied with adjusting to your new marriage. You can't take the place of a real parent, so don't try. Just give the children time to get to know you and make clear your concern for their happiness. Sooner or later they will accept that you are here to stay, and ready to be their friend. (See "Remarriage and Children," page 17.)

The potential for problems is there, but so is the potential for a richer, fuller life for everyone concerned. No difficulty is insurmountable when people really want to make things work. "It's a matter of sensitivity to all the children first," says one mother of an eight-year-old and stepmother of her husband's three teenage sons. "You have to realize that children deserve the presence in their lives of everyone who loves them, and that they should not be shunted back and forth, waylaid and forgotten, just because of adult frictions." There's no room for jealousy and resentment in an extended family situation—not if you want to make it work.

Dealing with children and former spouses will require patience, understanding, and maturity. Yet most couples in remarriage situations find that they emerge all the stronger for the conflicts they resolve together and all the more committed to making their marriage work.

Matters Legal and Otherwise

We've already pointed out that marriage is a public profession of a private commitment. The full impact of what that really means may not be felt until long after the wedding is over, until you start dealing with the world as a couple. Besides your personal promise to each other and your relationship within the privacy of your own home, you will have to recognize your new status as a married person under the law. This involves a great deal more than you might initially expect.

What Marriage Means—A Legal Definition

It is the active presence of government that gives marriage its formality in law. Although we usually think of wedlock as a relationship between two people, precisely the reverse is true. Marriage ends a two-party relationship by bringing in government as a third and dominant partner. Any two people can live together, but only a man, a woman and a state can make a marriage.[11]

According to the American Bar Association, almost anyone can obtain a license to marry. Generally, one must be over eighteen years of age or have parental consent (states vary), must be free of syphilis, and must not be a close relative of the intended spouse. The laws of every state forbid bigamy and do not recognize homosexual marriage.

While there is no written marriage contract as such (except for prenuptial agreements—see below), the act of marrying in front of witnesses and signing the license puts the contract into effect. As a civil procedure, marriage implies mutual benefit and financial support, assumes cohabitation (though does not require it), and ensures the legitimacy of any offspring resulting from the union. Some states even decree sexual fidelity, although rarely are such laws enforced.

In principle, this sounds simple enough. In practice, however, the whole area of family law is plagued by vagaries of interpretation and variances in state laws and statutes. The more complicated our lives get, it seems the more court precedents are required to deal with them. Because most married people have little if any idea what the laws in their state say about grounds for divorce, inheritance and property rights, alimony, child custody and support, or any other real or implied marital agreements, dissolution of a marriage through divorce or death often becomes a horrendous ordeal.

Marriage is terminated by divorce or death, but it may also be annulled (or "voidable"). Again, states vary, but a marital contract can usually be declared null and void if it can be proven that there was intent to defraud or absence of intent to marry from the very beginning. Annulment has been sought in cases involving failure to consummate the union, marriage under duress, or other cases of misrepresented intentions.

In spite of all the publicity about marital discord, marriage is considered publicly and privately to be sacrosanct. Law enforcement officers, social welfare agencies, and even friends and neighbors are reluctant to interfere in the private affairs of husband and wife. In some cases, like spouse abuse and domestic violence, this reluctance has thwarted justice and restricted individual freedom. In marriage, the burden of dealing with a bad situation almost always falls to the victim, as it does in most other civil and criminal procedures.

The main legal benefit of marriage, besides imparting legitimacy to children, is the assumption of some property rights to a surviving spouse in the event of death or divorce. These rights can also carry certain liabilities, however, so it is wise to know the laws of your state before making major ownership and inheritance decisions. Few states still recognize common-law marriage (automatic marriage after a period of cohabitation and after having "held one's self out to the world" as married), but many legal professionals view the advent of palimony suits as an extension of the common-law concept.

For more information about marriage laws in your area, write to your state bar association. You can also obtain a catalogue of booklets and other informational materials by contacting the American Bar Association, Order Fulfillment, 1155 E. 6oth Street, Chicago, Ill. 60637.

The Marriage License

Most states require marriage licenses, though the specifics of obtaining them do vary. In general, you will need proof of age or parents' consent, proof of citizenship if not American, and certificates of verification for blood tests and any other required physical examinations. Once the license is acquired, there is a waiting period before the license is valid and a maximum time period for its validity. Call your county clerk for specific state requirements, and plan to obtain the license two to three weeks before the wedding.

The marriage license is a legal formality. Although the red tape can be cumbersome, there is very seldom any difficulty in obtaining a valid license.

Prenuptial Contracts and Agreements

The main thrust of most prenuptial contracts is to establish the inheritance rights of both partners. A marriage partner is entitled to some property in all states, but prenuptial contracts usually extend or diminish these rights. A prenuptial contract supersedes both inheritance law and a will, and few courts have voided existing prenuptial contracts that have been correctly written and executed.

The concept of prenuptial agreements is not new. It has been used for many years by older couples or couples of widely differing ages, either in first marriage or remarriage, to safeguard accumulated property and/or the inheritance rights of children or grandchildren. It has also long been used by very wealthy individuals to protect their holdings acquired before the marriage. What *is* new, however, is the increasing use of prenuptial agreements by younger couples and by those marrying for the first time with nothing but their hopes and dreams to protect. The high divorce rate and the rapidly changing and frequently challenged state divorce laws seem to account for the rising popularity of such contracts.

There are both advocates and critics of prenuptial agreements. Some see them as a sort of insurance policy against the unforeseen and as a way of achieving openness and honesty in marriage. Others see them as destructive of love and trust and as unfairly protective of the wealthier spouse. Such agreements have proven effective in eliminating future misunderstandings in the event of divorce or death, and have ensured more equitable distribution of rights and property in states where the laws are biased or particularly unclear (including some so-called equitable distribution and community property states).

Basically, there are two kinds of contracts: the formal, legally binding agreement that deals with real material and financial matters; and the more or less behavioral agreement that stipulates roles and rights. No court in the world is going to rule on who does the dishes, for instance. So a distinction must be made as to the validity of the contract and the way in which it is executed. A do-it-yourself agreement will probably not hold up in court, and any contract that could be found to be *contra bonus mores* (against good morals) or against public policy in your state would also be invalidated. (Some states, for example, will not allow a waiver of alimony, no doubt out of fear that a destitute wife will become a welfare mother.)

If your premarital agreement is to be of any real value, here's what legal experts suggest:

1. Know the laws of your state. Make sure your contract will be considered fair and reasonable under the laws.
2. Each of you should have your own attorney to protect you against future accusations of fraud and to ensure that your best interests as an individual are looked after.
3. Be sure the agreement is in writing and that all finances and holdings have been disclosed.
4. Do not sign the contract under duress.
5. Realize that the contract will be only as good as the parties involved. (The other party can always contest it later, and could win.)

In addition, most lawyers recommend that an agreement should end after a certain number of successful years, that it be set aside after the birth of a child, and that it be rewritten in the event of a substantial change in the couple's financial status.[12]

Even if you decide that you don't want or need a prenuptial agreement, talking about some of the issues involved in a legal contract can be very beneficial.

Retaining Your Family Name

The custom of assuming a husband's surname came about because married women had no legal rights of ownership or personhood until the Married Women's Property Acts were passed in the 1800s. Until then, a married woman was legally her husband's chattel and assumed his name to indicate that she and all her possessions belonged to him. Interestingly enough, in the continental United States, taking your husband's surname has always been just a custom, never a law. (Hawaii was the only exception, but their reversal went into effect in 1976.) Since the women's movement, many state laws have been reinterpreted and liberalized to make it easier than ever before for a woman to maintain her maiden name after marriage.[13]

Sometimes retaining your family name is a practical matter; sometimes it's a matter of personal preference. A woman who has a substantial personal or professional reputation under her family name may find it easier simply to retain it. A woman who sees her name as a reflection of her identity might elect to retain her name for that reason or might incorporate her name with that of her spouse (Diane Smith Jones, or Diane Smith-Jones). Some men have also adopted a hyphenated surname (Joseph Smith-Jones) or have taken their wife's name as a middle name (Joseph Smith Jones).

Regardless of what you decide to do or how you decide to do it, you have a legal right to use your family name forever, no matter how many times you may marry. Don't let anyone dissuade you if that's the way you want it. A raised eyebrow now and then or the comment of a skeptical relative is no reason to acquiesce.

You should know that the Equal Credit Opportunity Act of 1974 gives you the right to use your own name on all joint accounts and loans. Insurance companies will hold policies in different surnames, though you should make it clear that you are married and entitled to family plans and benefits. Social security is not affected, since your number remains the same, nor does the IRS care about differing surnames as long as the tax return indicates you are married. You also have the right to retain your surname on wills, driver's licenses, voter registrations, and all other legal documents.

The birth of children does not affect your choice either, at least not on the actual birth certificate, since the mother's maiden name always appears. But in some states there may be a request for clarification if the child is not to carry his father's name. Persevere! Many couples alleviate the confusion by combining surnames for the child or by giving the child his mother's or father's surname as his middle name.

If you are at ease about keeping your name, others probably will be too. You can casually inform friends and family of your intention before the wedding, and you can use your own name on announcements and stationery after the wedding. Maintenance of a family surname is much more commonplace today than it used to be. For more information contact: Center for a Woman's Own Name, 261 Kimberly, Barrington, Ill. 60010.

Till Death . . .

"I just can't believe the way John is acting about our wills," moaned Nora, thirty-six. "We have children, property, investments—we have to have wills. He's being so childish, and he ought to know better. After all, he *is* a lawyer!"

His profession notwithstanding, John suffers from an irrational fear of admitting his mortality by writing a will—and he's not alone. Hundreds of thousands of people, people who should know better, die intestate (without having made a will) every year. They leave their families and loved ones heir to monumental red tape, exorbitant legal fees, unnecessary taxes, and additional anxiety simply because they, the deceased, would not deal with the inevitability of death.

Newlyweds with few assets may not need wills right away. But as soon as property starts to accumulate (a home, investments, etc.), wills should be drawn.

It is highly recommended to have a will, particularly when anything of value is owned or there are minor children involved. If you die without a will, possessions are scattered according to the state's determination of degree of kinship, and some state inheritance laws can be pretty archaic.

Unless there are vast holdings or unless there are children or other dependents involved, it is best to keep a will as simple as possible. Most couples name each other as heirs and executor(rix). What with the hourly rate of most lawyers today, this is not the time to add pages and pages to be sure Aunt Henrietta gets your set of silver spoons or your best friend receives the gold chain she's always admired. Just let your spouse know about any special wish, and trust him enough to take care of them should need be.

Because wills must be in compliance with state statutes, your will should be drawn up by an attorney licensed in your state and signed by the required number of witnesses. Out-of-state wills can sometimes lead to complications, so if you move, take existing wills to an attorney in the new state for verification. While it is difficult to generalize about fees, it will probably cost between $75 and $150 to have the forms drawn.

Drawing a will is never a pleasant task, but it is a practical necessity. Most of the time it is a pretty routine procedure. With a little objectivity and a good attorney, you can handle it.

Making a Home

*M*aking a home together is an exciting experience. While older married couples may moan and groan when the carpet needs replacing or the upholstery is worn, the two of you will delight in the shopping and planning that go into setting up your first home. Whether you're decorating a studio apartment or a ten-room house, you'll want your new residence to reflect the tastes and personalities of the two of you; you'll want it to offer all the comforts of home. (See "Bridal Gift Registry," page 30.)

Bridal market analysis tells us that nuptial couples account for $13.6 billion spent annually on setting up house. The average couple during the twelve-month bridal period (six months before the wedding and six months after) spends $3,070 on tableware and cookware, appliances, linens and textiles, furniture, and accessories. That makes you a pretty important customer! For a breakdown of how those dollars are spent, see the table on page 197.

Of course not all couples have this kind of money to spend, but even those who don't will enjoy shopping for bargains and exercising creative thinking to turn their house into a home. Many couples already own some furnishings of their own and take special pleasure in the challenge of integrating their belongings, a decorating feat so representative of what marriage is all about.

Whatever you have to work with, and however much you have to spend, consider these interior design tips when planning the decor of your first home.

The Cost of Setting Up House

Category	Total Sales Projected Yearly (in billions)	Average Per Couple
Furniture and home furnishings	$2.9	$1,160
Audio and video equipment	0.8	304
Home appliances	1.2	493
Tableware	0.9	370
Home textiles	0.7	272
Table accessories and holloware	0.6	219
Kitchen electric	0.3	130
Cookware	0.3	122
TOTAL	$7.7	$3,070

NOTE: These figures include the cost of gifts received by the couple, in addition to items they purchased themselves.

SOURCE: 1983 Bridal Market Study conducted for *Modern Bride* by Trendex, Inc., and Beta Research Corporation

- Buy the very best you can afford in major furnishings. Be sure items are well-constructed so that they will give you comfort and pleasure for many years.
- Choose styles and colors that reflect you both—your needs, your preferences, your way of life. Try to stay away from the decidedly masculine or feminine unless that is what you both like. A well-decorated home mirrors the personalities and interests of its inhabitants.
- Every room should have a focal point. Decide what it is to be and decorate around it. If it is an architectural detail, such as a fireplace or a picture window, then arrange your furniture to take advantage of the coziness or the view. If you have no architectural focal point (as so many new homes don't these days), then make one. Decorate a room around a smashing painting or an attractive wall unit. You can even build a whole color scheme by drawing out the shades and tints in a beautiful piece of decorative art, thereby making the art your focal point.
- If your first home is an apartment with limited space, you'll want to consider multifunctional furnishings that do not overcrowd tight quarters. Select easy-care pieces that can withstand daily use and entertaining needs. Modular sofas are very versatile, and modular entertainment centers can be expanded with additional audiovisual equipment as your budget grows.
- Painted Oriental trunks are ideal for storage and look wonderful as cocktail tables; a cantilevered chrome-and-glass sofa table can be a bar, a dessert center, and a display top. Because of their flexibility, simple furnishings like these make a natural transition into subsequent homes.
- Don't overlook the importance of accessories in pulling all design elements together. A blue sofa, beige chairs, and a brown rug can become remarkably unified when acented by an autumnal arrangement of dried leaves, tree bark, and blue cornflowers.

Setting up your first home together is a rewarding and challenging enterprise. And you don't have to do it all at once. You can budget and plan and experience the satisfaction of finally acquiring something you've both wanted. The gift registry can help you over the long haul too. Some stores notify former brides whenever their patterns go on sale, and they keep registry files available so that relatives and friends will be sure to give you gifts you'll appreciate on anniversaries and other special occasions.

Best of all, you have a lifetime together to grow and change, to blend tastes and recognize needs. You have a lifetime to create that special haven called home.

Renting an Apartment

There's more to consider when renting an apartment than just cost and location. Unfortunately, many couples with hectic lives and an overriding eagerness to get settled neglect the details that could become sources of problems and discomfort later.

"The wedding was getting closer and Ray and I were panicked. We just had to have a place that was convenient to school and work and that was something we could afford," explains Cheryl, a graduate student at a large eastern university. "I guess you could say we were sort of pressured into a decision. Now we're paying for it."

Ray and Cheryl have paid for it all along. During their first hot summer together, they discovered that "paid utilities" did not include an air-conditioning hookup and costs. When a fuse blew, they discovered that they didn't have access to their own fuse box and that the building super didn't live in the building. When Ray got a promotion and Cheryl graduated earlier than expected, they discovered that it would cost them their security deposit plus the last month's rent to break their three-year lease. Moreover, all the improvements they had made—bookshelves, carpeting, shutters—would have to stay behind. Ray and Cheryl were stuck for at least another eight months.

Asking the right questions and reading the fine print in the lease are crucial to making a wise decision. What is included in the monthly rent—water, electricity, gas, parking, garbage collection? How long is the lease? Can it be broken? Can the apartment be sublet? Can the rent be raised unexpectedly? What improvements are you allowed to make, and what maintenance can you expect to receive?

You'll also want to consider other practical matters. Are there laundry and storage facilities, security provisions, workable plumbing and appliances? Does the structure seem to be in good condition, and is it free of ants, roaches, and other household pests?

Finally, you'll need to know about the other tenants and the surrounding area. Is there a residents' association or a sense of community in the neighborhood? What kinds of activities are available—or prohibited? Are there restrictions against children or pets?

This list of questions may seem extensive, but all the questions are worth asking because they all directly affect your comfort and security in your own home. If you find yourself locked into a lease that restricts your life or stuck in an apartment that does not meet your basic living requirements, your new home will represent more of an aggravation than a respite.

To be sure, we all have to make compromises. Perhaps the supermarket is a little farther away than you'd like, but a quiet residential area is worth the inconvenience. Maybe you're not allowed to put up wallpaper, but you are guaranteed a fresh paint job in your choice of colors when you renew the lease. Like everything else, a rental decision comes down to individual priorities, to what is most important to your own happiness and comfort.

When investigating rentals, keep in mind that in some communities a couple can well afford the mortgage on a small house or condominium for the same monthly payments that rent would entail. Renting does mean an attractive freedom from certain maintenance chores and costs, but ownership provides tax advantages and the opportunity to begin building equity for the future.

Only the two of you can determine what's just right for you. If you're lucky, you'll know it when you see it. What an exhilarating feeling to be absolutely sure as you announce together, "We'll take it!"

Buying a Home

Owning one's home is a cornerstone of the American dream. America was one of the first nations in which every man had the right to own land, and today we still take great pride in exercising this right. Rare is the newlywed couple who doesn't speak and dream of owning their own home. And a surprising 38 percent of them already do when their marriage begins!

Economic uncertainties, high interest rates, and escalating property values have made realizing this dream difficult for many in the last few years. The potential home buyer has had to become a shrewd businessperson, keenly aware of fluctuating markets and astutely informed about financing alternatives. No longer is it sufficient simply to save and dream; timing has become a key factor in home-purchase planning.

According to the National Association of Home Builders, the average cost of a newly constructed single-family house in 1983 was $89,400. From the National Association of Realtors, we learn that the 1983 resale average (of preexisting single-family homes) was slightly lower—$83,000. While some communities are more expensive than others, housing costs in general have increased all across the country. The median existing single-family house is now worth $70,300 (NAR figure).

Numbers like these have shifted many couples' dreams away from the single-family home to the co-op or condominium. In this market, prices are generally lower and some home maintenance chores are assumed by the management—a real boon for the busy working couple. The condo or co-op offers a way of easing into the housing market without assuming a large debt, but with a probable return on the investment dollar. Equity and assets are accumulated and can be reinvested later in a more expensive property. "The condo has become the starter home for newlyweds," says one real estate broker, "and cooperative living is the wave of the future."

Whatever you decide to buy, you will probably need to see your friendly banker or other lending institution for a home mortgage. Acceptance of your mortgage application will be based on six factors: your present income, job stability, credit references, the size of the down payment you plan to make, your other material and financial assets, and the resale value of the property you are purchasing. Most lenders will also consider career potential—that is, the stability of the career field you've chosen and your anticipated salary growth.[14] In other words, lending institutions are in the business of money, not real estate. They want to be sure you can carry your loan and won't default on your obligations. They really don't want to have to repossess and resell your house.

To this end, you too should be realistic as to what size mortgage debt you can reasonably carry. Depending on your own debt ratio (the amount of your monthly income that's already allocated), your monthly PITI (principle, interest, taxes, and insurance) should fall somewhere between 28 and 36 percent of your real (net) monthly income. This is the general rule of thumb that banks use, and you would be wise to honor it as well. The interest and taxes are the most fluctuating components of this formula; they are the figures you will have to watch to determine when to buy.

Obviously, the greater your principle (the amount you borrow), the greater the interest and monthly payments. You will usually be expected to put up 10 to 20 percent of the purchase price as a down payment, and it may or may not be advantageous to put down more if you have it. Some good personal financial advice is in order for this decision. Some special mortgages allow less of a down payment (FHA or VA, for instance), but you will have to meet special qualifications for them.

In a fluctuating economy, you will probably also be asked to put down so many points (from one to three is standard) at the closing in addition to any bank service charges or application fees you might already have paid. A point is 1 percent of the amount of the loan (one point of $50,000 would be $500, two points would be $1,000, etc.). The number of points and other bank fees vary, so it pays to shop around.

You will also have to shop for the best interest rates. Banks and lending institutions in the same community can be very competitive. Economists are hoping that interest rates will remain fairly stable, in the 9 to 13 percent range, after the horrendous highs (19 percent) in 1981. But fluctuation in the marketplace and competition among lenders make it imperative that you compare and negotiate. Even a quarter of a percent can make a difference in your monthly payments.

Finally, you'll have to decide what kind of mortgage you want. If you need to be assured of the same monthly payments year after year for the twenty-five or thirty years of your loan, you'll want to secure a fixed rate mortgage. (If rates fall drastically, you can always renegotiate the loan.) If you are willing to gamble on the economy or if you feel sure you will resell the property in a short time (two to five years), then you may wish to investigate the many variable or adjustable rate mortgage plans available. Talk with your banker.

If you have a sound financial picture and a history of responsible financial performance, you probably will be able to secure a home loan. Moreover, with good financial credentials, you are in a position to negotiate. A young couple just starting their lives together represents future business for any lending institution, so loan officers should be just as eager to secure your mortgage as you are.

There are many excellent books and articles available through which you can learn more about debt financing and property evaluation. (See the Bibliography for some suggestions.) Home ownership is the single greatest financial responsibility most couples ever undertake, so it is wise to do the homework involved.

Living with Family

Amy and Burt had it made—or so they thought. They had dated for a long time, had a solid relationship built on equality and communication, and had even saved together for a down payment on their own condominium. The only snag in their plans occurred when they were informed that completion of their new home would be delayed by about three months. Since their wedding date was already set, they opted to save themselves the aggravation of finding a short-term apartment lease and to accept Burt's parent's offer to move in with them for the interim.

As is not uncommon with new constructions, bad weather, labor problems, and supply shortages turned a delay of three months into nine. By the time Amy and Burt moved into their own home, Amy questioned whether they "had any marriage left to move." They would have to soothe hurt feelings, salvage broken ties, and try to recapture the spirit of communication and partnership they had enjoyed before the wedding. For Amy and Burt, living with family was a disaster.

Such arrangements seem to spell disaster for most couples. Whether it's adult children returning home or aged parents moving in, adding members to an existing family household is bound to cause strain. For newlyweds, whose marital stability and couplehood depend on the independence they cultivate in the first year or two of their married lives, the family nest can be stifling.

Some couples, like Burt and Amy, don't realize the magnitude of the interpersonal challenges they face. Other couples may for one reason or another have no choice. Think carefully before making your home with either set of parents or with other relatives. If you decide to do so, sociologists and family counselors agree that the following considerations will make the arrangement more workable.

- Start with a family meeting. Make sure that all rights and responsibilities, financial and otherwise, are delineated and that an approximate time limit for the living arrangement is set. People will get along better if they know how long the situation is going to last and if each knows what is expected of him within the household.
- Respect each other's rights to privacy. Adults, especially newlyweds, need space for themselves, freedom to come and go, and areas in which to entertain friends and to pursue hobbies and interests. The best arrangement is that in

which common living quarters are not shared and separate entries are provided (like the mother-in-law suite or the two-family house).

- Keep personal discussions and problems personal. Not all matters between the two of you are subjects for family involvement.
- Finally, and this is a tough one, remember that it is *not* your house. The people who own it have a right to make the rules. If you move in, you'll have to accept that.

Multigenerational living patterns are becoming increasingly common in America, and that's not all bad. Many couples with aged or single parents adopt such arrangements and live quite happily and harmoniously. If your decision is based on choice rather than necessity, it is apt to have more positive results.

Moving In

Whether you'll be moving into his place, he'll be moving into yours, or you'll both be moving into a brand-new residence, relocation will be involved. Moving is seldom easy and almost always hard work, but what better reason to go through the hassle than to begin a new life together!

Actually, with a little advance planning and some good organization, you won't find relocation such a hassle. In fact it can even be fun. You would not be the first couple to have a moving party with family and friends who provide the brawn while you provide the beer.

That's one way to do it. If you aren't moving very far and if you haven't too many belongings to transport, moving yourself may be your best bet. Just be sure you have plenty of boxes on hand and a good-natured friend with a truck or van. Moving day could turn into a memorable social occasion.

Even if you have to hire a truck or trailer, a do-if-yourself move can be the most economical, perhaps costing half as much as a commercial move. Just don't underestimate the time and energy it will take.

If you have a long distance to go or many personal possessions, you'd probably be better off getting a professional to do the job. You'll want to get at least three estimates of the cost (most estimates are given free, but check to be sure) and specific information on insurance, delivery guarantees, redress for damages, and past performance records. (A referral from a satisfied customer is always a plus.)

The Interstate Commerce Commission regulates all interstate moves, and some states have their own regulatory agencies overseeing intrastate transportation. The Household Goods Transportation Act of 1980 has made it possible for some industry innovations that foster competition and protect the customer. One such innovation is the practice of binding estimates. Bidders will give you a fixed cost based on pound-weight estimates, and you'll have no surprises when you pay the bill.

Moving professionals are usually quite willing to help you keep costs down. They might suggest that you do your own packing (though you may be liable for damages) or that you share a load with someone else moving in the same general direction from your area. Investigate alternatives before making any firm commitments.

If you'll be moving far away, recognize that long-distance relocations at any time in life can be very traumatic. While it can be very good for a newlywed couple to learn to depend on each other and themselves in a new and different environment, there can also be moments of loneliness and homesickness. You can minimize these adjustments by finding out all you can in advance. The local chamber of commerce can provide information on the social, recreational, educational, and employment opportunities available, and a subscription to the local newspaper can give you a feel for the community. A personal visit or two before you're in residence would also help.

It takes time to feel at home in a new community. Explore. Get out and learn your way around, take advantage of the unique opportunities the area has to offer. Pretty soon your loneliness will disappear and you'll have friends and experiences you never knew existed.

For more information about moving, write for the free pamphlet titled "Your Rights and Responsibilities When You Move," available from the ICC, Room 5321, Twelfth and Constitution Avenues N.W., Washington, D.C. 20423.

Epilogue
Your Challenge for the Future

We are privileged to live in one of the most exciting eras man has ever known. Space travel, mass communications, and scientific discovery are no longer the domain of science fiction. They are the stuff of everyday life. In such a free and enlightened atmosphere, our relationships should be richer and fuller than ever.

There are those who say that increased life expectancy, greater freedom of choice, and the faster pace of our existence make lifelong fidelity to one partner unreasonable and obsolete. Times and people change, they argue, and nobody can promise anything forever.

Certainly we are all well advised to be cautious in making promises. But to suggest that it is impossible to share a lifetime of love, growth, and change with another person in a committed relationship is to refute the basic premise of marriage. Someone who truly believes that would be foolish even to attempt marriage in the first place.

To prove their point, the skeptics cite divorce statistics and discuss the traumas of extended families and single parents. Yet even a brief survey of history will reveal that divorce was always with us in numbers proportionate to the population. The only difference was that it wasn't documented as divorce but was called desertion or separation instead. Networks of families and friends have always come together to lend support to the single parents in the community, and hardly any of us can exhibit a family tree uncomplicated by stepchildren and remarriage.

Regardless of all the social and technological changes, couples want the same thing today as they always have: to be happy. Men and women have always viewed commitment with seriousness and anticipation, and they have always hoped to find love and fulfillment in their marriage. Though settings and circumstances may differ, modern couples are no exception, their chances for happiness no less real.

Every era has its challenges: time and patience seem to be ours. Because we have so many demands on our time, we tend to be stingy about sharing it and very impatient with anything that threatens to waste it. Yet patience over time is essential to the kind of growth and development a lasting marriage requires. If we give up too easily, if we refuse to allot the time and exercise the patience the other person deserves, we will forever flit from one relationship to the next without real rewards.

There are enough successful marriages around, enough landmark anniversaries, to prove that a good and lasting union between two people in love *is* possible. No one will tell you it's easy; no one will say it just happens. But happy couples will admit that their relationship has always come first, and that it has been the source of strength and support for individual accomplishments. "Without him or her," you will often hear the partners say, "I could never have done it."

On February 14, 1984, Reverend Jack and Gertrude Miller were interviewed on *People Are Talking*, a local television show in Baltimore, Maryland. The occasion? The Millers' sixty-first wedding anniversary. Reverend Jack was asked the secret of being married sixty-one years.

"Just keep telling 'em you love 'em," he replied, "and tell 'em and tell 'em and tell 'em."

Notes

Part One: Your Engagement

1.   Eric Fromm, *The Art of Loving* (New York: Bantam Books, 1956), p. 47.
2.   Merrill Sheils, "A Portrait of America: Death of the Family?" *Newsweek*, January 17, 1983, pp. 26–27.
3.   Alvin P. Sanoff, "Marriage: It's Back in Style," *U.S. News & World Report*, June 20, 1983, p. 50.
4.   "Here's What You Say About Marriage," *Seventeen*, May 1983, p. 92.
5.   The ritual of solemnized or blessed engagement is available in the Roman Catholic faith, through chaplains on some college campuses, and as a finale to the Engaged Encounter weekends.
6.   Betty Friedan, *The Second Stage* (New York: Summit Books, 1981), p. 57.
7.   Ibid., p. 66.
8.   Jean Seligmann with Rebecca Boren, "The Coupling of America," *Newsweek*, September 19, 1983, p. 75.

Part Two: Your Wedding

1.   Erma Bombeck, "New Beginnings Deserve New Underwear," *Stamford Advocate*, September 6, 1983, Sec. C.
2.   Based on a 1981 Eastman Kodak survey, but substantiated by subsequent market research. Eastman Kodak Company, Corporate Communications Division, Rochester, New York.
3.   Marcia Seligson, *The Eternal Bliss Machine* (New York: William Morrow, 1973), pp. 51–52.

Part Three: Your Marriage

1.   Ronna Romney and Beppie Harrison, *Giving Time a Chance* (New York: M. Evans, 1983), p. 12.
2.   Jonathan Gathorne-Hardy, *Marriage, Love, Sex & Divorce* (New York: Summit Books, 1981), Appendix G, p. 340.

3. Maxine Abrams, "Love, Sex and Marriage: Past, Present and Future," *Ladies' Home Journal*, January 1984, p. 70.

4. Kahlil Gibran, *The Prophet* (New York: Alfred A. Knopf, 1926), p. 15.

5. Joint Center for Urban Studies of MIT and Harvard, "The Nation's Families 1960–1990," as contained in John Naisbitt, *Megatrends* (New York: Warner Books, 1982), pp. 233–234.

6. John Naisbitt, "Megatrends for Women," *Ladies' Home Journal*, January 1984, p. 84.

7. Philip Blumstein, Ph.D., and Pepper Schwartz, Ph.D., *American Couples* (New York: William Morrow, 1983), p. 53.

8. While efforts are underway to change the situation, as of this writing, married couples filing jointly or singly still pay more in combined income tax than do two single adults with the same income.

9. The Kiplinger Changing Times book *Make Your Money Grow* is one of the best paperbacks around, and is now in its fifth printing by Dell. Also informative are the timely articles on current fiscal issues to be found in *Money* magazine and other popular periodicals.

10. Author Maggie Tripp did an excellent series of money management articles in *Modern Bride* running from the February/March 1979 issue to the December/January 1980 issue. Check your library.

11. Leland S. Englebardt, II, *Living Together: What's the Law?* (New York: Crown, 1981), p. 10.

12. Shelby White, "Personal Finance: Signing a Contract Before Marriage," *The New York Times*, September 25, 1983, Section 3, p. 11.

13. Two states still require a special precaution: Hawaii requires that a woman sign the name she intends to use on her marriage certificate, and Alabama requires her to fill out a special form.

14. Ruth Rejnis, "Buying a Home: What to Consider," *Modern Bride*, December/January 1984, p. 126.

Selected Bibliography

Thoughts on Life

Blumstein, Philip, and Pepper Schwartz. *American Couples*. New York: William Morrow, 1983. An eighteen-year study of American couples—how they live, think, and work.

Cassels, Louis. *What's the Difference? A Comparison of the Faiths Men Live By*. Garden City: Doubleday, 1965. A well-known UPI columnist's discussion of the similarities and differences in the world's major religions.

Enos, Sondra Forsyth, and Clive Enos, Ph.D. "Portrait of the American Woman." *Ladies' Home Journal*, January 1984, pp. 123–124, 179–181. A portrait of American women's lifestyles based on an unprecedented 86,000 responses to a *Ladies' Home Journal* questionnaire.

Friedan, Betty. *The Second Stage*. New York: Summit Books, 1981. Well-known feminist goes beyond feminism.

Fromm, Eric. *The Art of Loving*. New York: Bantam Books, 1956. The landmark philosophical treatise on love.

Gathorne-Hardy, Jonathan. *Marriage, Love, Sex & Divorce*. New York: Summit Books, 1981. A broad historical overview of how men and women come together and what drives them apart.

Gibran, Kahlil. *The Prophet*. New York: Alfred A. Knopf, 1926. A classic of poetic philosophy covering a range of human subjects and activities.

Krantzler, Mel. *Creative Marriage*. New York: McGraw-Hill, 1981. Well-known author and psychologist talks about marriage in the eighties and identifies the stages through which every marriage evolves.

Naisbitt, John. *Megatrends*. New York: Warner Books, 1982. A discussion of ten new directions in American life.

Pietropinto, Anthony, M.D., and Jacqueline Simenauer. *Husbands and Wives*. New York: Times Books, 1970. A nationwide survey of marriage based on a representative sample of 3,880 respondents.

Romney, Ronna, and Beppie Harrison. *Giving Time a Chance*. New York: M. Evans, 1983. Insightful and inspirational portraits of successful marriages.

Rothman, Ellen K. *Hands and Hearts: A History of Courtship in America*. New York: Basic Books, 1984. An entertaining and fully documented account of love and marriage between the Revolution and the First World War.

Ryan, Kevin and Marilyn. *Making a Marriage*. New York: St. Martin's, 1982. An informal conversation through which the authors share their own marital experiences and what they have learned from others.

Seligson, Marcia. *The Eternal Bliss Machine: America's Way of Wedding*. New York: William Morrow, 1973. A humorous, satirical look at American wedding traditions.

Sheehy, Gail. *Passages*. New York: E. P. Dutton, 1976. An analysis of the personality and sexual changes we go through in adult life.

Sheils, Merrill. "A Portrait of America." *Newsweek*, January 17, 1983, pp. 20–33. A comprehensive look at Americans' living, working, and family patterns based on data from the 1980 U.S. Census.

Practical Matters

Brothers, Dr. Joyce. *What Every Woman Should Know About Men*. New York: Ballantine, 1982. An examination of the physical, psychological, and emotional differences between men and women by the popular psychologist.

Conran, Shirley. *Superwoman*. New York: Crown Publishers, 1978. For every woman who hates housework and needs to get organized.

Dickson, Elizabeth, and Margaret Colvin. *Laura Ashley Book of Home Decorating*. New York: Harmony Books, 1982. Ideas for decorating including the coordinating of fabrics and wall coverings for every area of your home. Instructions for painting, papering, and sew-it-yourself projects.

Englebardt, Leland S., III. *Living Together: What's the Law?* New York: Crown, 1981. Examines the rights and obligations of cohabitating couples and the differences under the law between marrying and living together.

Fernandez, Genevieve. *The ABCs of Decorating*. Garden City: Doubleday, 1982. An interior design fact book for beginners.

Francke, Linda Bird. *Growing Up Divorced*. New York: Linden Press/Simon & Schuster, 1983. Helps divorced and remarried parents understand the effects of divorce on their children's lives.

Gaylin, Jody. "When to Keep Your Parents Out of Your Marriage." *Glamour*, October 1983, pp. 112–116. Handling parental interference in early marriage.

Gittelson, Natalie. "Learning to Live With the 'Other Woman.'" *McCall's*, October 1983, pp. 58–65. A roundtable discussion between newly married women and a psychiatrist on the subject of mothers-in-law.

Johnson, Flora, for the American Bar Association, Division of Communications. "Law and Marriage: Your Legal Guide" (a booklet). Chicago: ABA Press, 1983. A helpful guide to all the various legal aspects of marriage.

Latner, Helen. *The Book of Modern Jewish Etiquette*. New York: Schocken Books, 1981. Jewish etiquette for all occasions, including weddings.

Leo, Jacqueline McCord. *The New Woman's Guide to Getting Married*. New York: Bantam Books, 1982. A wedding and marriage guide geared toward remarriage and the more mature, professional woman.

Lewin, Elizabeth S. *Financial Fitness for Newlyweds*. New York: Facts on File, 1984. A practical guide for getting a marriage off on the right financial foot.

Matlins, Antoinette Leonard and Antonio C. Bonanno. *The Complete Guide to Buying Gems*. New York: Crown Publishers, 1984. Takes the guesswork out of this important decision.

Miller, Theodore J., ed. *Make Your Money Grow*. A Kiplinger Changing Times Book, fifth printing. New York: Dell Books, 1983. A practical guide to managing money and investments.

Porter, John Paul, et al., eds. *How Things Work in Your Home (and what to do when they don't)*. New York: Time-Life Books, 1975. A practical, no-nonsense guide to what you can and can't repair around the house.

Porter, Sylvia. *Sylvia Porter's New Money Book for the 80's*, Volumes 1 and 2. Garden City: Doubleday, 1975, 1979. A simple, easy-to-understand discussion of every conceivable financial matter from budgets to bonds.

Rejnis, Ruth, and Carolyn Janik. *All America's Real Estate Book*. New York: Viking Penguin, 1984. A practical guide to the most common question and fears people have about real estate investment.

Routtenberg, Lilly S., and Ruth R. Seldin. *The Jewish Wedding Book*. New York: Harper & Row, 1967. The proper etiquette for and an explanation of the Jewish wedding rituals.

About the Authors

Since 1949, the editors of *Modern Bride* have provided engaged women with all the information they need during their hectic wedding planning months. Six times annually, under the direction of Editor-in-Chief Cele Goldsmith Lalli, *Modern Bride* presents the newest in wedding fashions and etiquette, romantic honeymoons, first home decorating, and the contemporary topics that concern couples today. The editors' combined experience in the bridal field totals more than seventy-five years—enough to get every couple off to a bright future.

STEPHANIE H. DAHL is an author and lecturer on marriage and family, and a regular contributor to *Modern Bride* and other national and regional publications. Originally from South Texas, she holds a B.A. in speech from Our Lady of the Lake University in San Antonio, and an M.A. in English from the City University of New York. Ms. Dahl now resides with her husband and son in Stamford, Connecticut, where she is still "writing and talking," and teaching nonfiction writing at Fairfield University.

About the Illustrator

JOANN WANAMAKER created the artwork for many of the advertisements for Macy's appearing in *The New York Times*. She has also done illustrations for *Vogue*, *Women's Wear Daily*, and various advertising agencies. She drew many of the illustrations in *What's What* by David Fisher and Reginald Bragonier, Jr., published by Ballantine Books in 1982.

JoAnn lives and works in New York City. In her free time she designs and sells lithographs of Fire Island, where she spends her summers.